Rhythm & Blues GUITAR

BY CORNELL DUPREE

Editorial assistance by Dave Rubin
Photos courtesy of Cornell Dupree

ISBN-13: 978-0-634-00149-9
ISBN-10: 0-634-00149-3

HAL•LEONARD® CORPORATION

7777 W. BLUEMOUND RD. P.O. BOX 13819 MILWAUKEE, WI 53213

Visit Hal Leonard Online at
www.halleonard.com

Foreword

There are certain names that one automatically associates with excellence in the realm of human endeavor: Muhammad Ali, Babe Ruth, Sir Laurence Olivier, Ella Fitzgerald, Wes Montgomery, B.B. King. Each exemplifies the highest achievement in their particular discipline. In the field of R&B guitar, one name shines like a supernova among the other stars-Cornell Dupree. R&B producer Jerry Wexler refers to him as "...the first guitarist I encountered who could simultaneously play rhythm and lead. Until then, we required two, sometimes three guitarists to handle those diverse functions." Since 1962, Cornell Dupree has come to represent all that is admired in that classic American music, including sophisticated and syncopated grooves, deep blues phrasing, and rich, vocal-like tone. A product of the Fort Worth, Texas blues scene from the late fifties, he went on to help reshape the world of Rhythm & Blues in New York with King Curtis in the sixties. Since then, he has not rested on his laurels; instead he's been constantly striving to improve and expand his musical vision with numerous solo projects and bands.

It is a great pleasure to be able to present Cornell and his unique approach to the art of R&B guitar. Everything you need to create your own style is here for the taking: the hip chord voicings, cool scales, tasty licks, and detailed instructions on how best to apply them. A CD is also included so that you can hear how the man himself plays. As an extra bonus, fascinating historical information about Cornell and the illustrious individuals that he has encountered over the years will increase your enjoyment as you delve into his music.

Dave Rubin
New York City, 2000

I would like to extend a special thanks to the people who influenced and assisted me in my career:

To the late, great King Curtis for bringing me to New York, being a big brother and a teacher.

To Jerry Wexler for my introduction to Atlantic Records.

A special thanks to Chuck Rainey for his friendship, support, and for always being there for me.

To all the artists whom I had the pleasure of performing and recording with.

A very special thanks to my lovely wife Erma and our three children James, Celestine, and Cornell III.

Thanks to Dave Rubin for his assistance and input with this project.

Cornell Dupree
New Jersey, 2000

About the Recording

The enclosed CD includes 10 songs written and performed by Cornell Dupree (with Dave Rubin on bass guitar). On the examples featuring two guitar parts, Gtr. 1 is mixed far left and Gtr. 2 is far right. In all other cases Gtr. 1 is mixed dead center. If you wish to play along with the recording, go to Track #11 for tuning notes.

Biography

Early Days in Texas

Not *all* the great blues and rhythm & blues guitarists are from Texas, but Cornell Luther Dupree is certainly one who holds that distinction. Born in Fort Worth on December 19, 1942 to Bernice and Cornell, Sr., he was raised an only child by his mother following the untimely passing of his father in 1944. He understands that his father had been an amateur guitarist who clowned around at parties. His grandfather, however, played country & western music on the fiddle at "hoe-downs" and at home. Cornell remembers picking up the fiddle and "sawing on it" when he was four or five years old, and he recalls his mother practicing gospel music on the piano to play in the church. The Dupree household also had an old Victrola, upon which popular music of the day would be occasionally played. Cornell mainly heard C&W music around his neighborhood at this time, and the only place to hear blues and R&B was on radio station KNOK in Ft. Worth between the hours of twelve and five in the afternoon. Artists like T-Bone Walker, Lowell Fulsom, Charles Brown, and Louis Jordan were popular in the black community then, but the great Texas guitarists like Walker and Fulsom did not yet appeal to young Cornell. Instead, he was attracted to the alto saxophone when he was eleven after seeing a local TV show that featured a catchy jazz tune played by the house band. Previously to this, he had figured out some boogie-woogie patterns and little tunes like "Boiling Cabbage" on his mother's piano. His mother bought him a saxophone and Cornell began private lessons with a junior high school music teacher in his home. The lessons lasted for a few years until he went to junior high and joined the school band to learn marching band music.

Getting a Guitar

At this same time, he had a friend who worked the concession stand at the local venues where R&B entertainers such as Little Richard, Ray Charles, and B.B. King would perform. Cornell would often accompany him to these engagements, and on one particular occasion got to see Johnny "Guitar" Watson at a Masonic Hall. Watson had a hit on the radio with "Those Lonely Lonely Nights," and Cornell was so taken with his playing and performance that he became tremendously attracted to the instrument and begged his mother to get him one. He also had two friends who played guitar, Frank Lott and Calvin Love, and was able to convince his mother of his seriousness. A used, sunburst acoustic Stella was procured at a pawn shop. Cornell began to learn to play it at the age of 14, even as he continued to play alto sax in the school band. His mother, who was always supportive of his musical interests, would occasionally take him to the clubs in the area to see local musicians. Edward Franklin, Huary P. Wilson, and a fellow known as "Catman" were some of the guitarists that Cornell came to know who would show him licks. Eventually, they began stopping by the house, calling him "little brother" and taking more time to instruct him. By this time, Cornell had to have an electric guitar, and his mother bought him a Harmony hollow body with a DeArmond pickup and a Silvertone amp for Christmas of 1956.

Cornell had become aware of the music of Jimmy Reed, Muddy Waters, Lightnin' Hopkins, and Little Son Jackson. He then started playing rhythm and boogie-bass figures with his guitar buddies, and the three of them, plus drummer Murphy Crockett, would play talent shows after school. In addition, some of the nicer neighborhood clubs allowed youngsters to come in and play on Sunday afternoons. Cornell and his fledgling group also received exposure and experience (and very little money!) in this manner as well. With Cornell on his Harmony, Frank on his Les Paul, and Calvin with his arch top Gibson, they played mainly blues and R&B instrumentals, including some originals.

From Blues to R&B

By now, Cornell had begun to make the distinction between "down home" blues and rhythm & blues. People he would place in the latter category would be singer Bobby "Blue" Bland and organist Bill Doggett. Their guitar players, Wayne Bennett and Billy Butler, respectively, had become the object of his admiration, and Edward Franklin showed Cornell some of the licks from Butler's classic solo on "Honky Tonk." Purchasing the 45 RPM recording of the hit instrumental from 1956, Cornell proceeded to learn it exactly in order to play it with his group on a Les Paul Custom. Unfortunately, the first good Gibson that he had acquired met an untimely end—it burned to an ash in its case when he left it overnight at a club that had a fire. This instrument was replaced with a Les Paul TV model with one P-90 pickup (see photo on next page). He had also started working with Huary P. (U.P.) Wilson, one of the other local guitarists who had tutored him when he first started to play. In this group, Huary used to play all the solos on Cornell's guitar (and would still show him licks as he had done earlier), and Cornell would play rhythm on Huary's Stratocaster. Called Kiel and the Boogie Chilluns, the band consisted of Cornell (who was the youngest) and Wilson on guitars, singer Robert Gaston, with bass, saxophone, piano, and drummer Robert Ealey, who was older and much more experienced. Richard Kiel was not in the band, but was the "manager" who got the gigs locally within a 200 mile radius of Ft. Worth. It was often an adventure with everyone and the equipment all piled into one station wagon. Cornell recounts a trip to Abilene: "We were on our way to do a one-nighter and we got pulled over by the cops. Robert Ealey was driving without a license. I was sitting in the back and had my license. Ealey turned to me and asked for mine, and like a fool, I gave it to him. When he handed it over, the policeman asked how old he was. Of course, Ealey could not remember how old I was, and he said, 'Let me go ask my brother.' So, that was a bust; they confiscated all our instruments and he got a big ticket. We missed the gig; I also got a ticket and had to go back to Ft. Worth. I had to go downtown, and my license was suspended for several months. We had to go back to where we got stopped (between Ft. Worth and Abilene) and pay the fine to get our equipment back. Actually, we were not bothered all that much because it was a nice, well dressed band, and no one got rowdy. I didn't get rowdy because I was too young!"

Segregation

Like the rest of the country in the fifties, Texas was segregated in most aspects, with separate (but not equal) facilities such as water fountains, rest rooms, and eating establishments. Outside of black and white country folk getting together once in a while at hoe-downs, the races did not mix. The clubs that Cornell played in were not integrated yet, although he did occasionally play for white audiences. As has been true for too much of this country's history, black music was welcome and appreciated by whites, but black musicians were not. Cornell remembers having to come in the back way, or through the kitchen, and then leaving quickly when the gig was over. This began to change about the time he was with Leon (Childs) and the Hi Tones in 1958-59, as they regularly played in the white clubs to better personal treatment. At one particular place, the White Sands Supper Club, they played R&B dance music (such as Ray Charles's "What'd I Say") seven nights a week.

The Texas Scene

Though not as well known a hot bed for blues and R&B as Houston, the Dallas-Ft. Worth area was cooking in the late fifties and early sixties. Master musicians like T-Bone Walker, Lowell Fulson, and Wayne Bennett, along with local heroes Ray Sharpe, Frankie Lee Sims, Sonny Rhodes, ZuZu Bollin, and Earl Bell were part of the scene at some point. In addition, artists as diverse as Ray Price, Bob Wills, Roger Miller, and Ornette Coleman were spreading their considerable influence around. The blues was so accepted across

Cornell in Texas, January, 1960

the spectrum that a Ray Sharpe could be kept busy in the white clubs, throwing in the occasional C&W tune upon request, but mainly staying true to his roots. Cornell recalls the Skyline Ballroom was a focal point for Ft. Worth musicians, as all the bigger acts, like Bobby Bland and Ray Charles, would perform there.

In Houston, Albert Collins, Pete Mays, Joe Hughes, and the Green brothers (Cal and Clarence) were presenting swinging Texas blues. Also included in the Houston group were Lightnin' Hopkins, Fenton Robinson, Little Junior Parker, and Larry Davis, while in San Antonio Gatemouth Brown held sway.

The vitality of Texas blues has never really flagged. Though it's been given a shot in the arm every so often by the likes of Johnny Winter and Stevie Ray Vaughan, many of the originators mentioned still work the region.

King Curtis

While still with Leon Childs at the end of the fifties, Cornell began working with Louis Howard & The Red Hearts. He got married in 1959, and graduated from high school a year later at age 18. According to Delbert McClinton, he had by then acquired a reputation as one of the finest blues guitarists around. In 1961, he was playing a gig at the Paradise Club with Howard when he met King Curtis. Curtis was in Texas on a visit from New York and had stopped by to say hello to the owners, Erin and Robbie Watkins. Upon hearing the band, he asked to sit in. Over the course of his stay, Curtis sat in many nights and struck up an acquaintance with Cornell. Before heading back to the Big Apple, Curtis told Cornell "keep on practicing, and one of these days I will send for you."

In 1962, Curtis called the Watkins', who delivered the message to Cornell. He went by their house where a call was put through to Curtis in New York. Cornell was auditioned over the phone (!) for the gig by having to play Curtis' hit "Soul Twist" and the jazz standard "Moonlight In Vermont." He passed, and a plane ticket to New York was sent.

On Monday, October 1, 1962, Cornell took his first plane ride and arrived in New York City with his

Cornell with King Curtis on Soprano Sax

Les Paul and his wife, Erma, in hand. Their son James and daughter Celestine had remained behind with Cornell's mother and grandfather. He took a taxi to Curtis's house, and on Tuesday, October 2, he was playing at Small's Paradise in Harlem. Being as he only knew "Soul Twist," he had to learn the rest of the repertoire on the gig.

Cornell stayed at Curtis's home until he found a place of his own, and played full time in the band. Curtis was busy with bookings at Small's on the weekends, and out on the road, including trips to Canada. Within six months, Cornell attended his first recording session with the band, with Cornell's hero Billy Butler also playing guitar (ironically, it was Butler whom Cornell was replacing in the performing band). He also contributed to some of the songwriting (uncredited), as he would sit around with Curtis, who also played a little guitar, and figure out licks and arrangements. Cornell had exchanged his Les Paul for a Gibson ES-335 shortly after joining the band, and within a year had acquired a Guild Starfire like the one Curtis had.

Touring with Sam Cooke

Cornell remained with Curtis on a full-time basis from 1962 to 1966, during which time he added to his family with the birth of his youngest son, Cornell III in 1963. The band during those years included Ray Lucas (drums), Jimmy Lewis (bass), and George Stubbs (piano) along with Cornell and Curtis. They worked regularly at the most prestigious R&B venues like the Apollo Theater in Harlem, and with the biggest stars, including Sam Cooke. The King Curtis band backed up the legendary soul singer and the heart of his band, drummer Albert "June" Gardner and guitarist Clif White, in 1963 on the last tour he did before his tragic murder in 1964. Cornell remembers White showing him some chords and parts of Sam's songs, particularly the main themes to "Having A Party." The King Curtis band also functioned as the warm up for Cooke, as there was no opening act.

The tour took the band throughout the East and the South, with a sensational live recording being made in Miami, Florida in January. With the King Curtis band providing more "grease" than the backup Cooke usually had in the studio, plus the enthusiasm of a black audience, *Live At The Harlem Square* Club shows a side of the singer not previously revealed on record. Augmenting the regular group on this date was guitarist Bobby Womack, who had been performing with his brothers as the Valentinos. Like Clif White, Cornell remembers this tour as being loud due to the audience screaming for Cooke, with the results being that the musicians had a hard time hearing themselves. The extensive traveling necessary for a tour of this type left quite an impression on Cornell, while the exposure for the band led to more engagements. During 1964, they played the New Jersey shore resorts of Atlantic City and Wildwood. One of the big stars they opened for was Fats Domino, and Cornell, bassist Chuck Rainey (who had just joined Curtis), and Domino's guitarist Roy Montreal would sit around in the hotel room jamming for hours. One of the tunes that Montreal showed Cornell was "The Girl From Ipanema," thereby adding to his repertoire of standards. There was also another musician around on these gigs that Cornell hung out with during the off hours who would go on to some notoriety.

Playing with Jimi Hendrix

The Isley Brothers were often on these shows with King Curtis, and Cornell got the opportunity to meet and play with their guitar player as well. James Marshall Hendrix had joined the Isleys after they had seen him win first prize on amateur night at the Apollo Theater. Cornell and Jimi hit it off, and they would trade licks, especially ones involving string bending, and talk about their influences. Both men admired Albert King, and Jimi was also a fan of Elmore James and other country blues guitarists. By the end of 1964, he left the Isley Brothers and bounced around between Little Richard, Ike & Tina Turner, and Curtis Knight, a local New Jersey R&B singer. King Curtis remembered seeing him with Little Richard and offered him a spot beside Cornell, where he remained for the better part of 1965. As the band did not have a regular keyboard player at this time, Curtis felt that two guitars would fill out the sound. In addition, he was impressed with Jimi's showmanship and, as Cornell puts it, "he could play." Though a shy person, Hendrix was extremely serious about his guitar playing (and chasing girls).

Jimi's rise to ultimate fame could not be forseen while in the Curtis band, though Cornell recalls that he was a showstopper with his onstage moves and antics. The two guitarists never really worked out their parts, but Cornell just assumed the role of rhythm guitarist because "no one else was doing it." Eventually, Jimi's excessive volume and lackadaisical attitude towards showing up on time and being properly dressed led to Curtis firing him.

Opening for the Beatles

Ben E. King and Cornell Dupree

In 1965, the King Curtis band played with the Beatles at their historic Shea Stadium show in New York. Though it is not widely known, the King Curtis band, along with several other groups such as the Exciters and Cannibal & The Headhunters, also opened for the "lads" in Canada, Chicago, and Los Angeles. The experience was a highlight for Cornell, as the Beatles and all the other musicians had a great time hanging out on the plane rides, playing cards, and listening to music together. Cornell says that the audiences, for the most part, were respectful of the opening acts and appreciated what they were doing, even though they were extremely anxious for the Beatles. Curtis and his band were given one half hour to play, and he kept things moving along with a variety of songs.

Cornell was playing a thin line Standel with humbucking pickups through a blackface, pre-CBS Fender Twin Reverb amp at this time, though he held on to his Starfire. He and Curtis would have long conversations about his sound, as it always seemed muffled, and not as clear and sharp as was desired. It would take a while longer, however, for Cornell to finally hit on the combination that would provide his signature sound.

All the while, the King Curtis band worked non-stop. The stars of R&B that Cornell ran across during this time reads like a who's who of soul: Otis Redding, Gladys Knight, Ben E. King, Doris Troy, Solomon Burke, and the Coasters.

Back to Texas

Despite all the activity with Curtis, Cornell was dissatisfied with his situation. Since moving to New York, he had stayed in touch with people back home in Texas, especially Ray Sharpe. In 1966, he gave his notice to Curtis and moved back to Ft. Worth. Curtis tried to discourage him from leaving, as did his contacts at the Apollo, but to no avail.

Cornell began working with Sharpe and bought a home and car for his family. However, he remained in close touch with Chuck Rainey back in New York. Rainey had become busy with sessions, and one Christmas he went to Ft. Worth to visit Cornell and to try to talk him into returning to New York.

Back to New York and a "Rainy Night In Georgia"

In 1968, Cornell packed up and returned to the Big Apple, stayed with Rainey for a few months and eased back in with Curtis. A tour with Dusty Springfield and Brenda Holloway followed later in the year. He started picking up session work again, with some coming from Rainey, some from Atlantic producer Jerry Wexler, and some from guitarist Eric Gale. Cornell had met Wexler when the producer was involved in a live recording at the Apollo around 1965 that included the King Curtis band. Gale was the hot session guitarist in New York in the late sixties and was often overbooked, resulting in Cornell getting literally half of his dates. Over a period of time, by networking with new acquaintances and old ones from the Apollo Theater, Cornell was able to establish himself again.

Jerry Wexler was one of Cornell's biggest fans and he kept him busy—hopping around from Criteria Studios in Miami, to Fame Studios in Muscle Shoals, Alabama, and Atlantic's studios in New York. It was during one of his sojourns to Florida in 1969 that Cornell was featured on the recording that would catapult him to the top R&B guitar spot on the session scene. Backing Brook Benton on November 5, Cornell provided the smooth, memorable fills on Tony Joe White's classic "Rainy Night In Georgia"—in the process creating what would become the standard version of the melancholy ballad. When the record was released in 1970, the calls started flooding in for Cornell's services. Producers would want him to give them "one of those 'Rainy Night' licks." Meanwhile, Cornell was also in Muscle Shoals regularly, adding his brand of hip funk to the recordings of Aretha Franklin, Sam & Dave, Wilson Pickett, Eddie Harris, and even Petula Clark.

In early 1971 the King Curtis band backed Aretha for a live recording at the Fillmore West in San Francisco, followed by a European tour with Aretha that included the taping of a live album in Montreux, Switzerland behind the blues piano player, Champion Jack Dupree (no relation). Unbeknownst at the time, it would be the last tour that Curtis would make before his tragic death at the hands of a junkie in front of his apartment building in Manhattan on August 13, 1971. Cornell and Curtis had become very close friends over the years, with Curtis visiting Cornell back in Texas for vacations and Christmas. The death of this magnificent musician was a tremendous loss to the music community, and to Cornell personally.

After the King Curtis Band

Jerry Wexler continued sending work Cornell's way after the death of King Curtis as his admiration for the exemplary guitarist grew. In his autobiography, *Rhythm & the Blues,* Wexler describes Cornell as the first guitarist he heard who could play simultaneous rhythm and lead: before him they had to have two or three guitarists in the studio. Relying on Cornell as his "trouble-shooter," Wexler had him doing dates with artists ranging from James Taylor to Donny Hathaway. Hathaway had been brought to New York and Atlantic Records by Curtis. Cornell became good friends with him and ended up playing on all his major recordings, including a live album at the Bitter End. Other artists from this period that Cornell backed were Roberta Flack and Margie Josephs. For most of 1972 he was on the road with Roberta, and in December of that year he was involved in a bad traffic accident with her and Jerry Jemmott. After several weeks spent in the hospital recovering, Cornell went to the Caribbean Islands for some R&R. Upon his return in January 1973, he went back out on tour with Roberta. The aftermath of the accident, however, had left him with his playing abilities impaired, and in April Roberta reluctantly cut him loose from her band.

Signing with Atlantic Records

The two giants of R&B guitar: Cornell and Steve Cropper.
Cropper produced Stuff It *in 1978.*

While still recuperating and re-gaining his faculties on the guitar, Cornell was signed to a one-year contract by Atlantic Records in mid-1973. The result was his first solo album, *Teasin',* with his old friend Chuck Rainey co-writing and playing bass. The title track had been written by King Curtis for his album *Get Ready,* with Eric Clapton on guitar and Delaney Bramlett producing.

By this time, Cornell had formed a group of his own called Encyclopedia of Soul with Gordon Edwards: bass, Charlie Brown: saxophone, Keith Williams: vocals, and various drummers, including Herbie Lovelle. They played the club circuit in New York and took up a virtual residency at Mikell's. Local musicians would often stop by at the weekly gig and sit in. Two drummers who Cornell became acquainted with during this time were Steve Gadd and Chris Parker. By 1975, a new band had been born out of this collective group of musicians called Stuff. With Gadd on drums and Edwards on bass, Richard Tee was added on keyboards. In short order, guitarist Eric Gale was brought in along with second drummer Chris Parker. Managed by Just Sunshine Music, the group was taken to Warner Brothers and signed. Stuff was a funky instrumental outfit that garnered a fair share of success, particularly in Japan, where they were hugely popular. For the first time in his career, Cornell was receiving royalties on tunes he had written for the band, and their second album, *More Stuff,* was nominated for a Grammy in 1976.

Cornell holds gold record for More Stuff,
November, 1978

Stuff stayed together until 1979 despite the lack of full commitment from the various members who were involved in other projects at the same time. The demise, however, was mainly the result of an atmosphere of distrust brought on by management.

Los Angeles

Cornell had also been freelancing all the while, and continued to do so until 1982 following the breakup of Stuff. With session work in New York slacking off a bit, he decided to go west and "see what things were like on the other side." So, once again, Cornell and his family packed up and moved to Beverly Hills. Unfortunately, it proved not to be the most advantageous move at this time. According to Cornell, " I knew a lot of people in L.A., until I got there. And then, no one knew me." Calls to contacts like Quincy Jones, Stanley Clarke, and Billy Preston were made but not returned. "Catfish" and Dallas Hodge, however, hooked up with Cornell. Formerly with Bootsy Collins, they formed a group called Chicken Legs with Cornell and former Little Feat keyboardist Skip Van Winkle—playing clubs in L.A. and touring with Bonnie Raitt in 1983/84.

Ironically, Cornell began getting more calls for work back in New York than he was in L.A. One notable exception was a session that resulted in the theme song for the *Bill Cosby Show*. Finding himself commuting to New York more and more often, he made the decision to move again. Looking back on the whole West Coast experience, Cornell remembers it as a scene where a lot of jamming went on, with not enough real work of any substance.

Back to New York

In March of 1985, the Duprees changed addresses once again. Cornell recalls, "We looked like the Beverly Hillbillies," as they towed a trailer piled high with the family's belongings. Renewing his relationship with Gordon Edwards, he began doing "Stuff-type" jobs in the New York metropolitan area. Meanwhile, Steve Gadd was forming a new group called the Gadd Gang with Richard Tee, bassist Eddie Gomez, and Cornell completing the lineup. The band performed and recorded, and eventually added Ronnie Cuber on baritone sax. Like Stuff, they were immensely popular in Japan and in Europe, where they often toured.

Cornell relocated to Connecticut in 1986 as he continued his involvement with the Gadd Gang and assorted freelance projects, including a reformed Stuff with Gordon Edwards. In addition, he traveled to Japan on two occasions with saxophonist Sadoa Watanabi, and also worked with Herbie Mann. Keeping busy, in 1988 Cornell signed on with Island Records as a solo artist and cut the Grammy-nominated *Coast to Coast*.

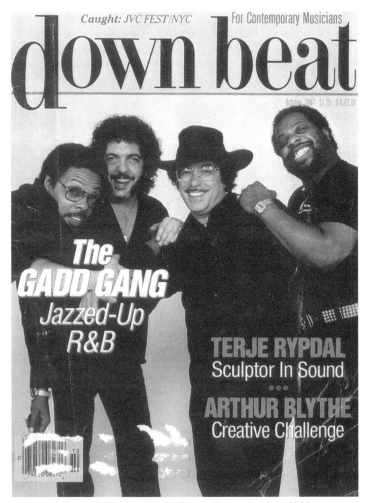

The Gadd Gang, Cover of Down Beat, *October, 1987.*
(L to R) Cornell, Steve Gadd, Eddie Gomez, Richard Tee

Back to Texas

Realizing that he was on the road a great deal of time anyway, the Duprees moved back to Fort Worth in 1990. He signed a contract with Amazing Records from Austin, produced two albums, and then went to Herbie Mann's Kokopelli Records out of Santa Fe, New Mexico. It was there that *Bop 'N' Blues,* his latest solo album, was recorded and released in 1995. He continued touring regularly with Herbie as well as with his own group called Who It Is. Comprised of Frank Canino on bass and Richard Tee, Chris Parker, and Lou Marini on saxophone, the band also found a receptive audience in Japan.

With very little work close to home and more calls coming from New York, Cornell once again, rounded up his family yet again for the move back East.

Back to the East Coast

In 1997, Cornell settled in Edgewater, New Jersey, across the Hudson River from New York City. Working with a pool of musicians that includes Chuck Rainey: bass, Bernard Purdie: drums, Lonnie Liston Smith: organ, and Bobby Watson: alto saxophone, known collectively as the Soul Survivors, he continues to perform locally and in Japan.

Heading into the 21st century, Cornell Dupree is at the top of his game as a musician. With no contenders in sight, he is still the premier R&B guitarist of his generation.

Playing the Blues

Hearing Johnny "Guitar" Watson back in Fort Worth, Texas made me want to play the guitar. He could really bend those notes. Though I am known as an R&B guitarist, I come from the blues, and it is my roots. Before we get to the blues songs on the CD, I want to give you some background into my style.

Blues Chords

Here is a selection of chords that I use when playing blues. You don't need a lot of fancy chords to play the blues, just the right ones. Here are some chord forms in the key of G. Learn these and you will be well on your way.

I Chords:

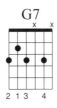
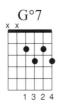

IV Chords:

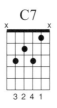
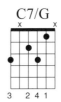

V Chords:

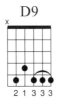
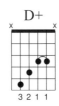

Blues Scales

I mostly use three boxes from the blues scale. Here they are in their basic form in the key of G.

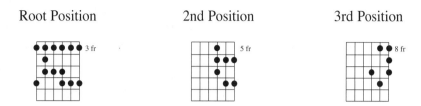

Root Position   2nd Position   3rd Position

I also add notes from the Mixolydian mode to the blues scale. This is sometimes called the "composite blues scale."

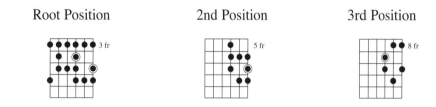

Root Position   2nd Position   3rd Position

Occasionally, I use notes from the major, diminished, and whole-tone scales, although I mainly save them for R&B, funk, and jazz. I like the whole-tone scale for augmented chords.

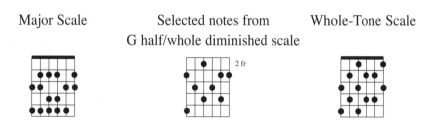

Major Scale   Selected notes from   Whole-Tone Scale
G half/whole diminished scale

J.R. Shuffle

This is what I call your basic "Jimmy Reed Shuffle." What I have tried to do is capture the feel of his songs and the way he would sing. Since I do not sing, I let my guitar "sing" the vocal part. You will notice that even though there is a boogie shuffle rhythm track, I still insert chords into my solo. It is a trademark of my sound, no matter what style of music I happen to be playing at the time.

Musical Analysis

- Boogie patterns with added chord tones are used for the I, IV, and V chords.

- The E blues scale is used for improvisation.

- There are subtle quarter-step and half-step bends on the ♭3rd. In addition, there are several half- and full-step bends on the fourth that provide sophisticated, bluesy tension.

- Unlike most blues guitarists when playing in the key of E, Cornell doesn't make use of the root position of the blues scale between frets 12 and 15 at all.

◆ J.R. SHUFFLE

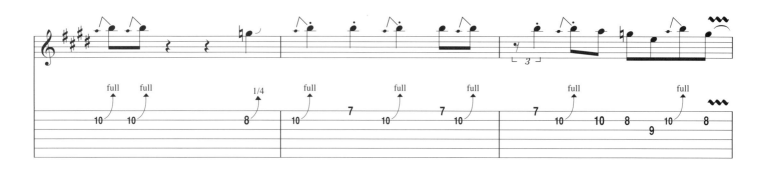

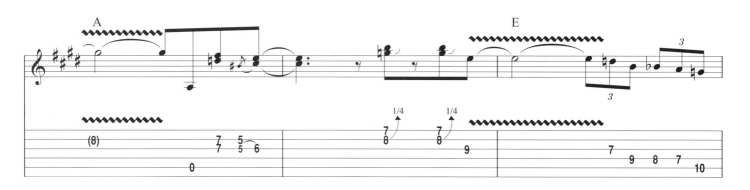

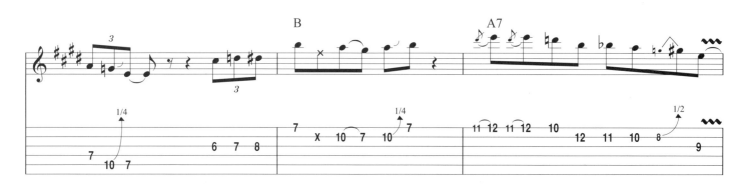

Gtr. 2: w/ Rhy. Fig. 1, 1st 10 meas., simile

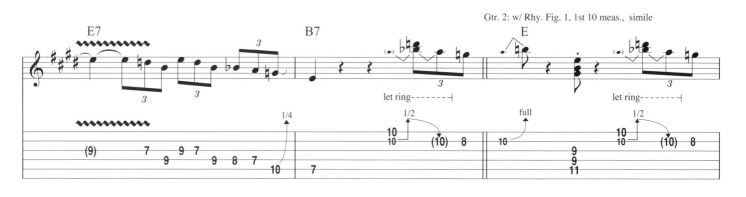

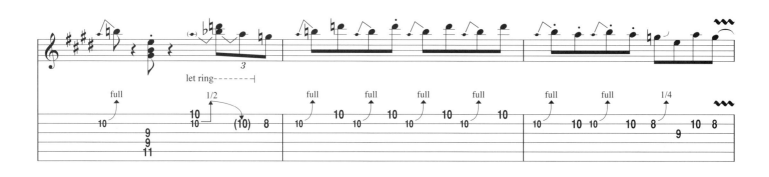

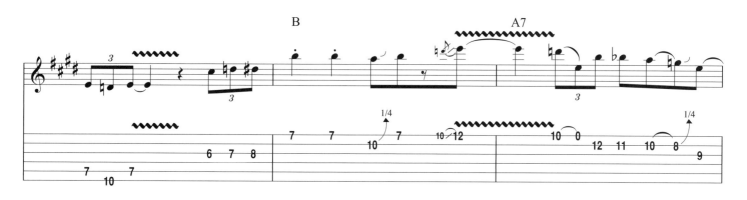

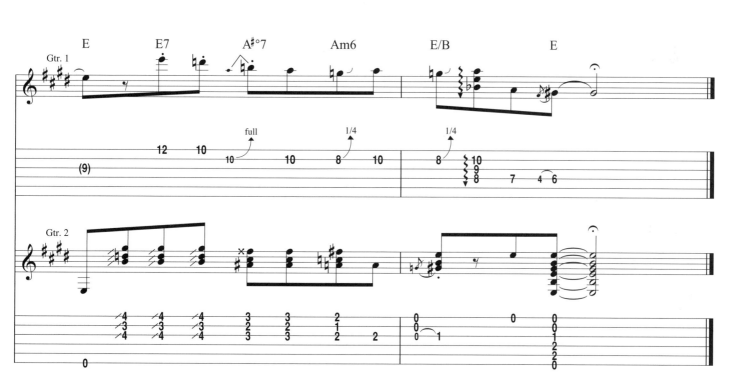

Plain Ole' Blues

Like everyone who came up in the forties and fifties, I was eventually influenced by T-Bone Walker. I really liked the way he played slow blues, and I still use the 7th and 9th chords that I heard in his music. I tend to play fewer notes than a lot of other blues guitarists anyway, but I believe it is especially important to leave a lot of space in a slow blues. Be sure to put a lot of feeling into each bend and vibrato.

Musical Analysis

- 9th chords are used for the I and IV chord changes. A dominant seventh chord is used for the V chord in measures 9 and 12, while a V+ chord substitutes for the I chord on beat 4 in measures 3, 15, and 27.

- Instead of the IV chord appearing in measure 10, the ♭VI substitutes on beats 1 and 2 with the V chord on beats 3 and 4.

- Diminished chords are inserted into the standard I-IV-I-V turnaround in measures 11 and 12. The musical tension they provide resolves to the I and V chords, respectively.

- The G composite blues scale is used for improvisation. The ♭3rd and ♭7th notes are often bent one-quarter step to the "true blue" notes in between the ♭3rd and major 3rd, and the ♭7th and the major 7th.

❷ PLAIN OLE' BLUES

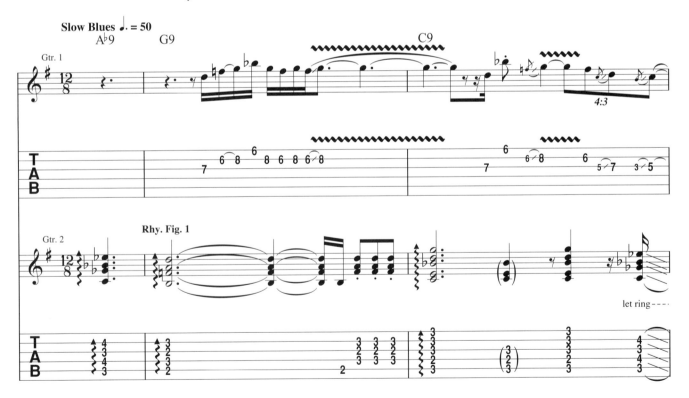

18

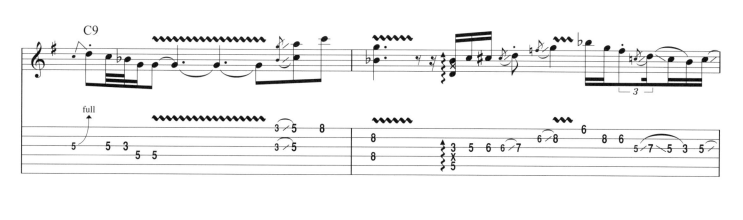

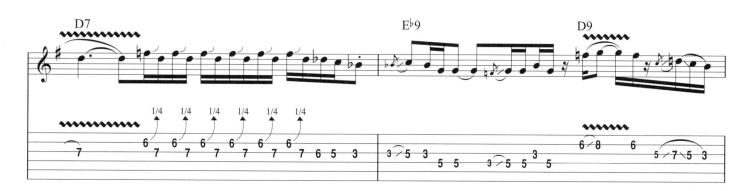

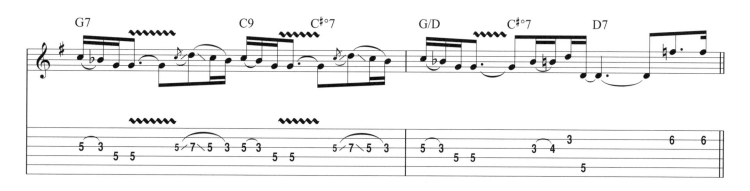

Gtr. 2: w/ Rhy. Fig. 1, first 10 meas., simile

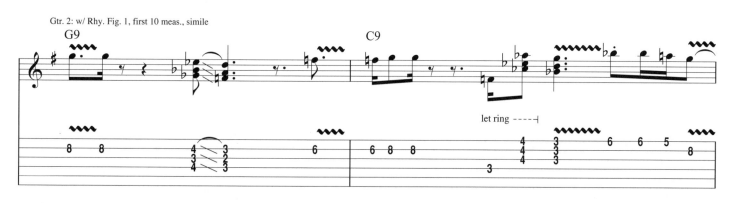

Swing Shuffle

Texas guitarists play a lot of swinging shuffles. I think part of the reason for that is the jazz influence in Texas music. My first instrument was the saxophone so I tend to phrase like a horn player. Notice how I try to develop themes and riffs throughout, especially in the third and fourth choruses. These are the kinds of sounds you might have heard a horn section play in Texas in the forties and fifties.

Musical Analysis

- Sliding dominant ninth forms, triads, and double-stops implying the IV7 and V7 chords are used for the rhythm accompaniment.

- The G composite blues scale is used for the solo. Both the ♭3rd and the major 3rd are played over the I chord at various times, providing musical tension.

- True "blue note" quarter-step bends occur on the ♭3rd and ♭7th.

- Sliding 6th-interval double stops in the solo help to emphasize the individual chord changes.

❸ SWING SHUFFLE

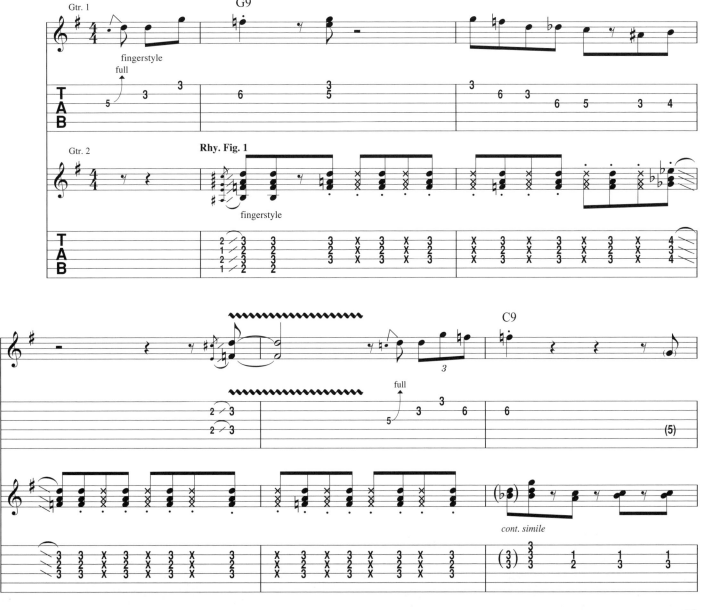

End Rhy. Fig. 1

Gtr. 2: w/ Rhy. Fig. 1, 2 times, simile
Gtr. 1

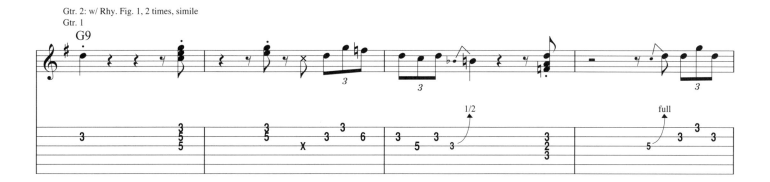

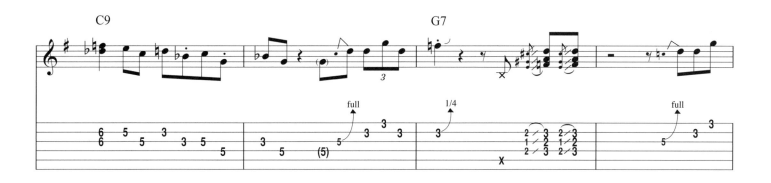

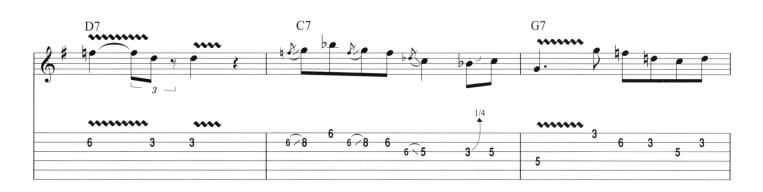

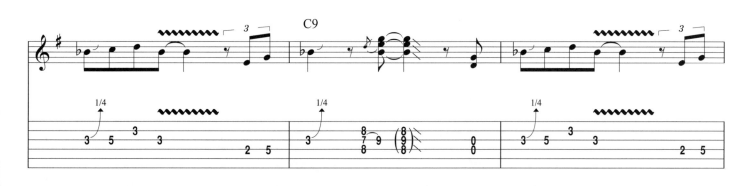

Gtr. 2: w/ Rhy. Fig. 1, 1st 10 meas., simile

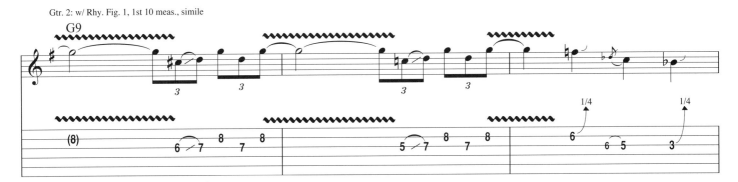

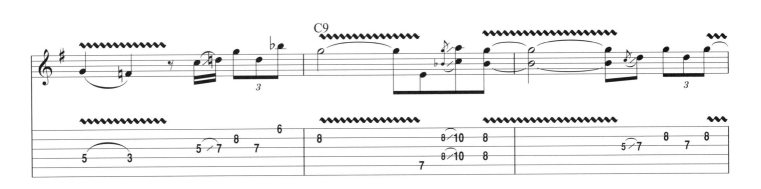

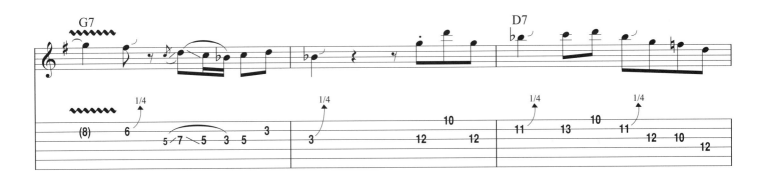

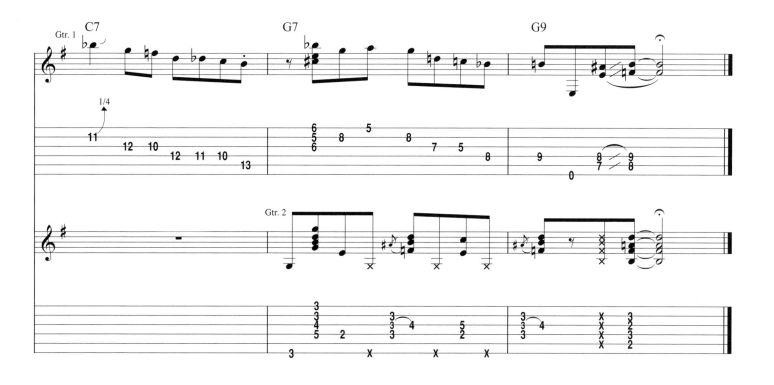

Minor Blues

I really enjoy playing a slow minor key blues because so much feeling can be put into it. I think that you should always make every note count when you play, particularly with a slow blues. With a slow minor key blues, you should leave as much space as possible and put everything you have into making each note expressive.

Musical Analysis

- Broken chord forms are used for accompaniment on the i (Am7) and iv (Dm7) chords. An E7 arpeggio is used for the V7 chord.

- The A minor pentatonic scale, with the addition of the 9th and ♭9th notes, is used for the solo.

- Double stops implying Am, Dm, and E are also included in the solo.

- Combination glisses and hammer-ons add a fluid quality.

❹ MINOR BLUES

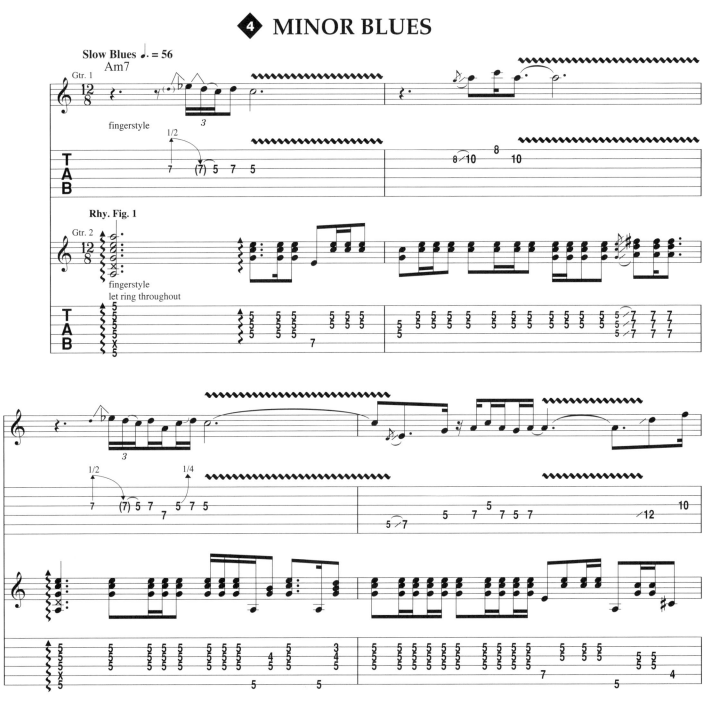

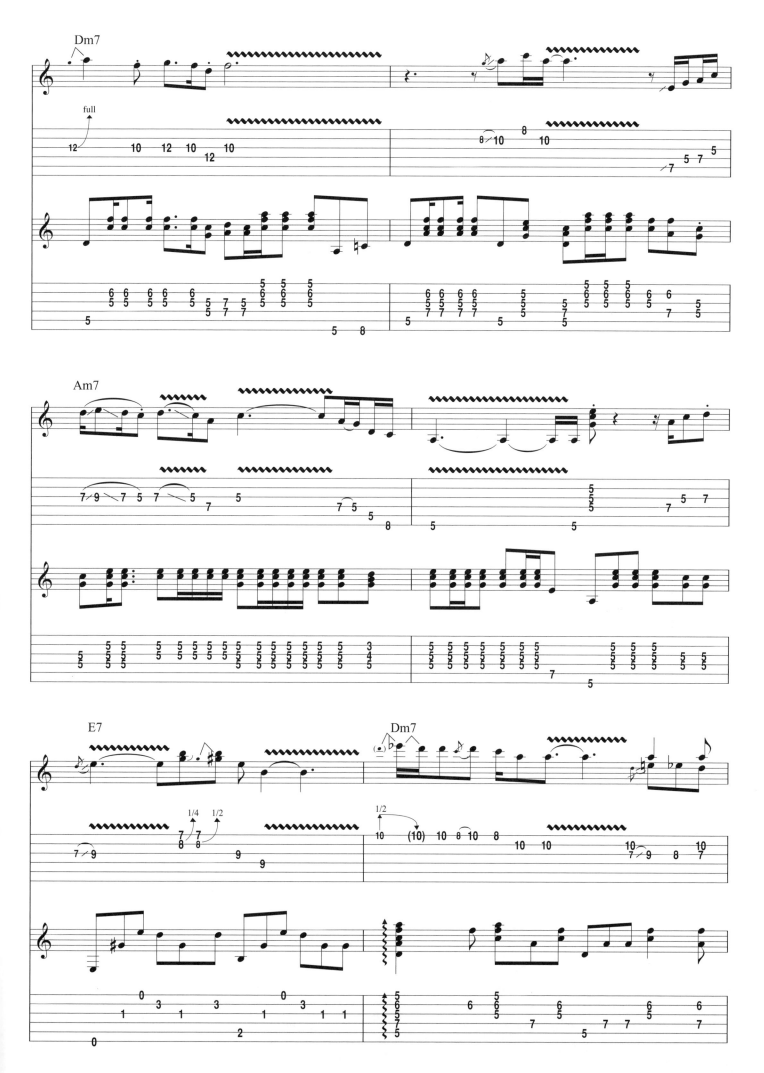

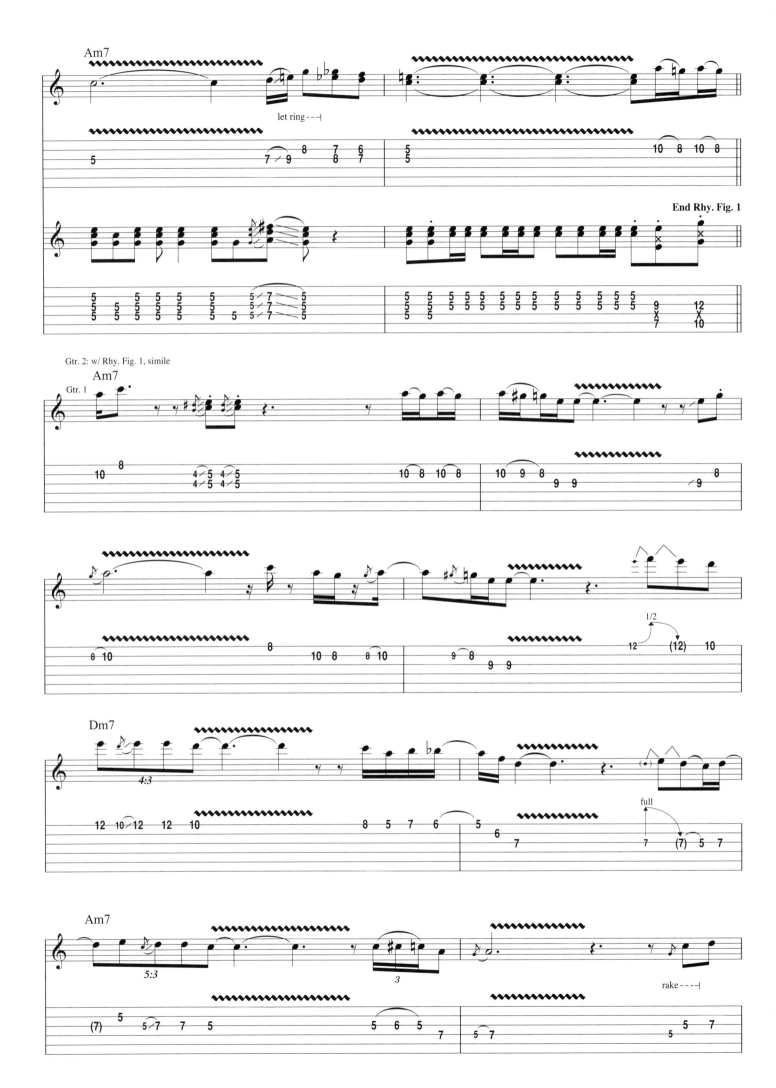

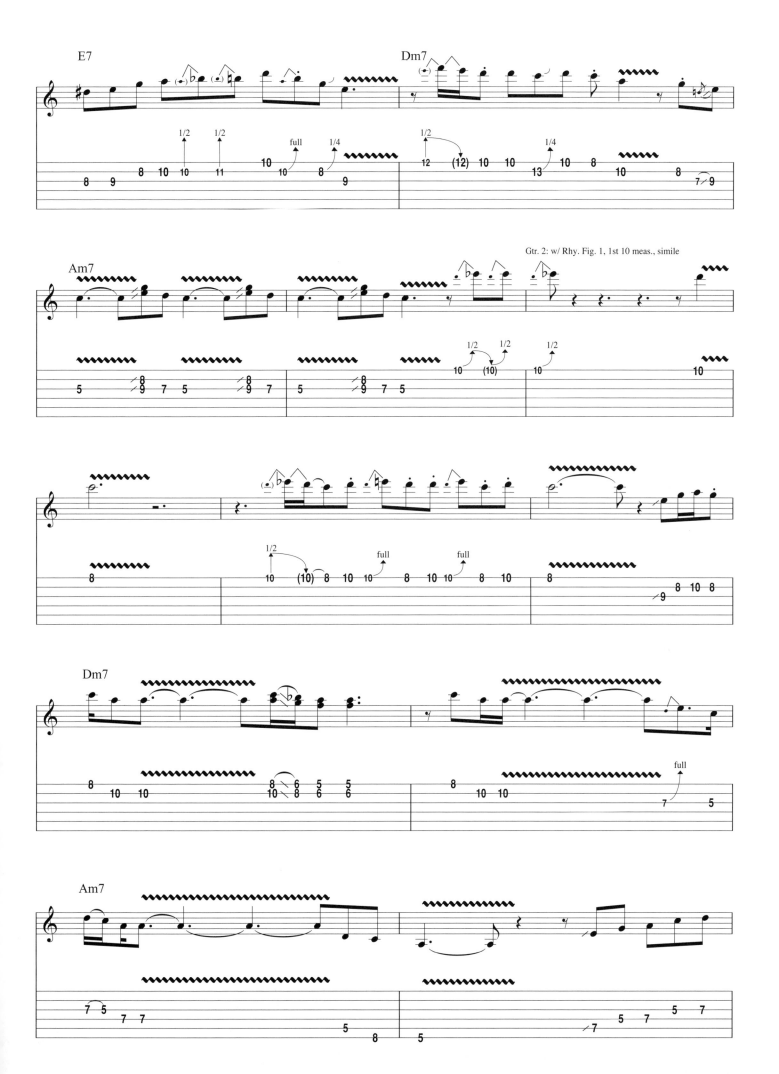

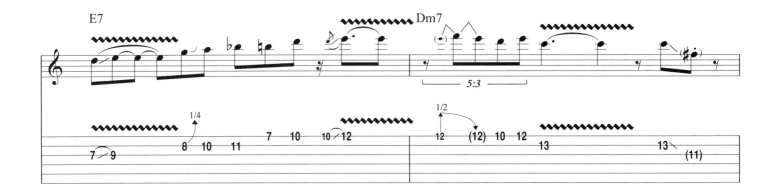

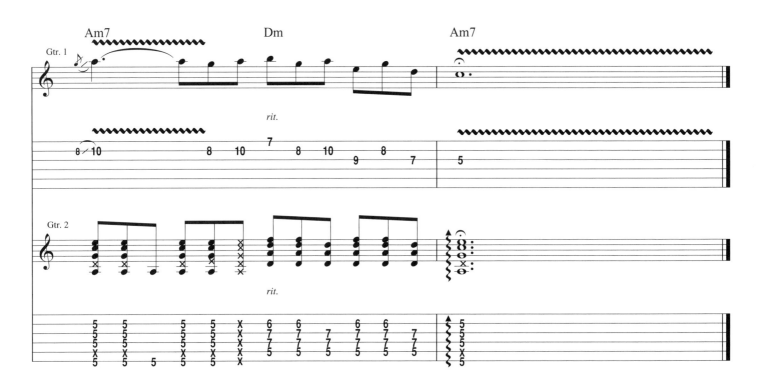

Rhythm & Blues Guitar

Playing guitar with King Curtis gave me the chance to not only learn to play R&B from one of the masters, but to also make my own contribution to the music. Though the blues has always been my roots, I have been drawn towards rhythm & blues. I think it is the best description of the kind of music I am known for playing.

As in the blues, there are certain chords that I favor for R&B. If you are not familiar with these forms, I recommend learning them before going further with the CD.

R&B Chords

As opposed to the blues, these chords can be interchangeable as I, IV and V chords (or others, such as II and VI).

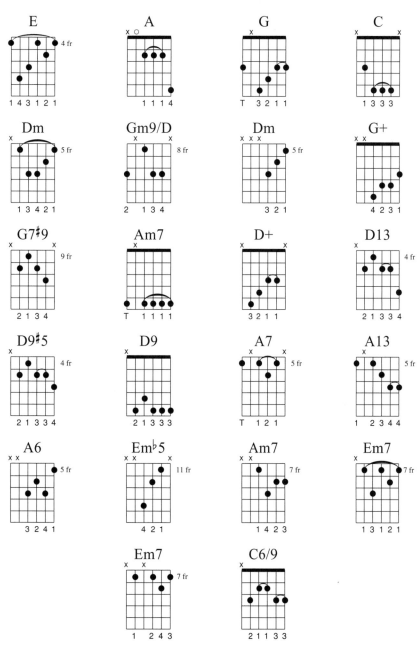

T = thumb

I-IV R&B Vamps

The heart of much R&B music is the chord change from I to IV. When these chord changes are used as a repeating pattern it is known as a "vamp." Often a I-IV vamp consists of one measure of the I chord and one measure of the IV chord. Here are a selection of I-IV vamps with some of my favorite chord voicings. The "X" under each chord frame represents one beat—4x = four beats.

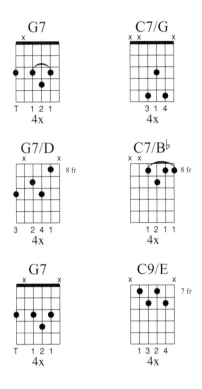

This one has a double stop connecting the I to the IV chord that is played for one beat.

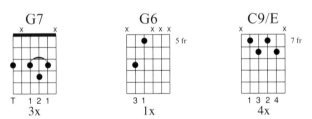

Soul Dance

Soul Dance has a I (E)-IV (A) vamp in sections A, C and D. This R&B tune is similar to arrangements I would do with King Curtis and shows how I would combine chords, bass licks, and riffs into one complete guitar part.

Musical Analysis

- The A and D sections consist of two 8-measure phrases. Each 8-measure phrase is constructed from four, 2-measure segments. Measures 7 and 8 in both phrases contain a "fill" with treble licks from the E composite blues scale and bass runs from the E major scale.

- The C section has one 8-measure phrase similar to the 8-measure phrases in sections A and D. Measures 7 and 8, however, have rapidly strummed double stops relating to the E chord.

- Sections B and E are eight measures long and have double stops relating directly to each I, IV, and V chord change.

- Section F remains on the I chord for the full eight measures and consists of a rhythmically strummed E7 chord for measures 1-4. Measure 4-8 have a humorous fill similar to "Shave and a Haircut, Two Bits."

❺ SOUL DANCE

R&B Double Stops

I use double stops along with licks to improvise. There are double stops in 3rds, 4ths, 5ths, and 6ths. I probably play double stops in 6ths the most frequently. They sound like "two-note chords" and are derived from scales. Here are some of the double-stop scales in 6ths that I use. They are all in the key of G Mixolydian and work well with dominant seventh chords.

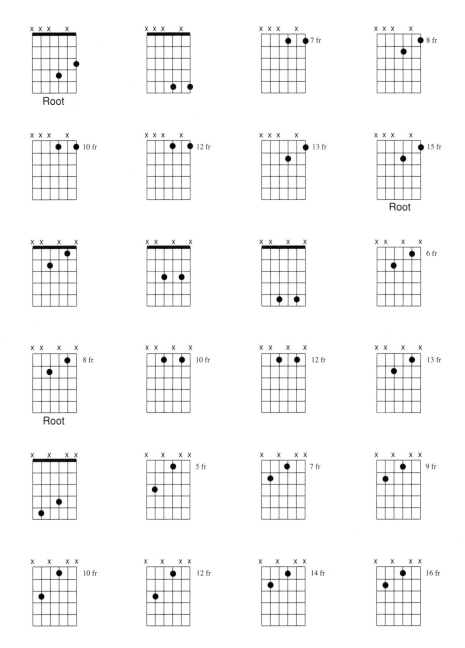

Soul Lullaby

Like "Soul Dance," "Soul Lullaby" is similar to songs that I used to play with King Curtis. It is also based on a I-IV vamp. Curtis would solo very melodically over my accompaniment that included double stops in 6ths, along with chords and bass notes.

Musical Analysis

- The arrangement consists of a 4-measure intro (section A), 20-measure verse (section B), and a long coda, or tag (section C), 31 measures in length.

- The intro contains a I-IV vamp.

- The 20-measure verse is based on I–IV–V changes arranged as follows: I chord – 4 measures of I (A♭)-IV (D♭), IV chord – 4 measures of I (D♭)-IV (G♭) based on the IV chord, I chord – 4 measures of I–IV, V chord – 2 measures, IV chord – 2 measures, and I chord – 4 measures of I–IV.

- Section C is also built on a I–IV vamp, however, a G♭ chord is inserted as a "grace" chord following the A♭ inversion (A♭/E♭) in measures 1, 3, 5, 7, 9, 11, 13, 15, 17, 19, 21, 23, 25, 27, and 29.

◆6 SOUL LULLABY

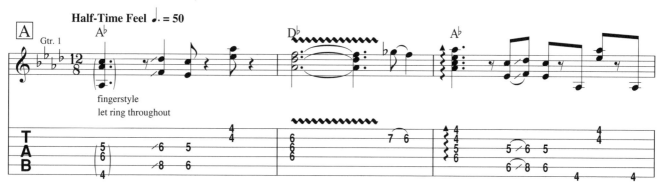

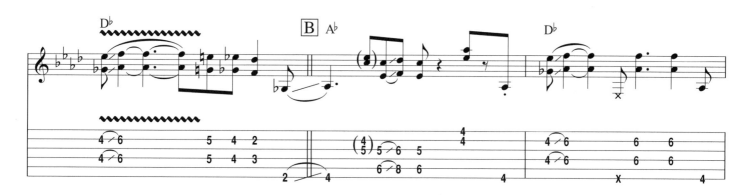

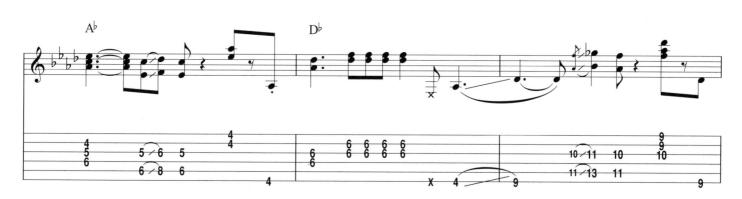

*Fretted w/ thumb.

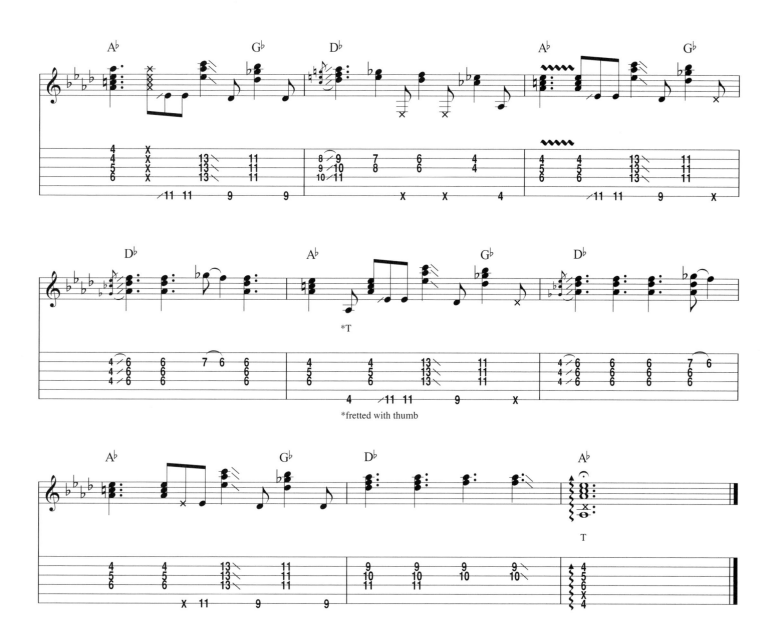

*fretted with thumb

I-VI-II-V Changes ─────────────

A common chord progression in R&B music consists of I-VI-II-V changes. Usually, the VI and II chords are minor. A lot of pop and rock music in the fifties used these chord changes to the point where they became a cliché. When played with the right R&B feel and more sophisticated voicings, however, this progression still can provide interesting challenges for improvisation.

Here are two ways that I play I-vi-ii-V changes in the key of C. The "X" under each chord frame represents one beat. 4X = four beats.

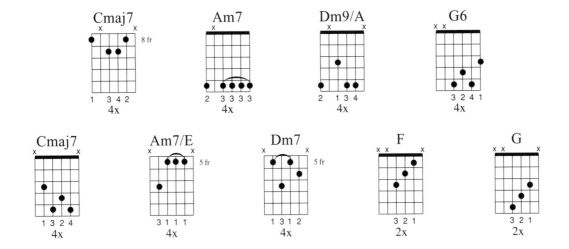

Ice Cream

I call this track "Ice Cream" because musicians have often jokingly referred to I-vi-ii-V progressions as "ice cream changes." Many jazz songs are based on these changes, however, and I have taken this opportunity to show the "jazz side" of my playing style.

Musical Analysis

- Each chord in the 2-measure I-vi-ii-V progression is played for two beats.

- The root position of the C major scale at fret 8 is used for the bulk of the improvisation.

- The root, 3rd, 5th, and 6th notes from the C major scale are emphasized.

- The 9th (2nd) is often bent up to the major 3rd. In addition, the ♭3rd is bent up to the major 3rd and the 6th is bent up to the ♭7th.

- Measures 26-30 contain octaves similar to Wes Montgomery and George Benson.

- The chordal accompaniment (Rhy. Fig. 1) contains double stops and partial chords, along with triads and 4-note voicings.

◆❼ ICE CREAM

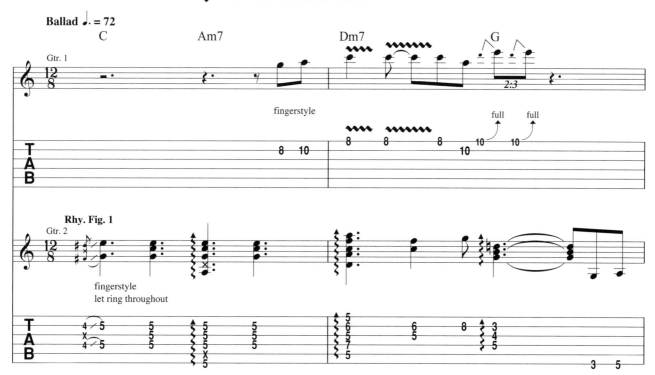

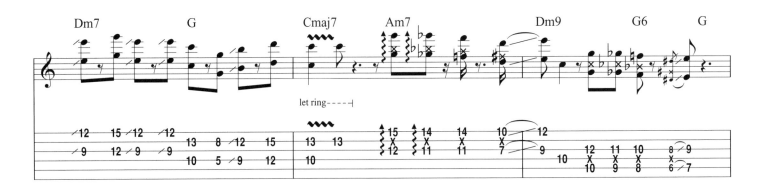

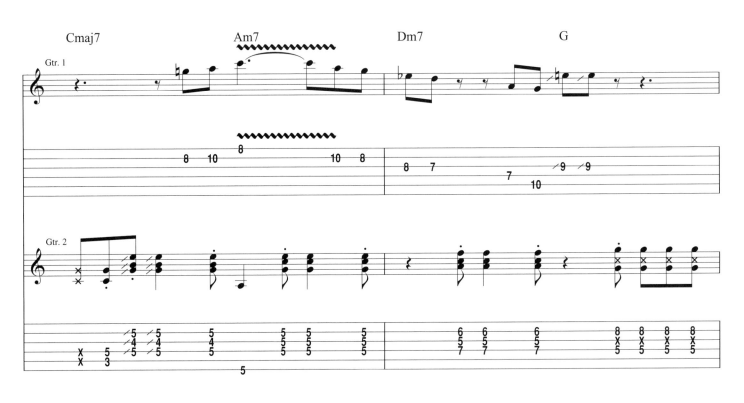

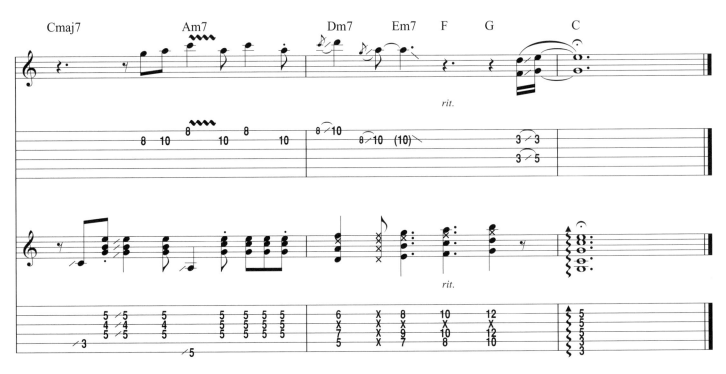

Funk #1

When I was with Stuff and the later bands I got to use my funk chops. "Funk #1" is based on a I-IV vamp and could be considered a backing track for other instruments or a vocalist. What I have tried to do is play a variety of licks and rhythms around the I-IV chords to show you some of the possibilities.

Musical Analysis

- The I (G9) and IV (C9) chords are played for two measures each throughout.

- Double stops and partial chords are used to embellish the 4- and 5-note chord voicings.

- The root note (G) of the key is often used as a bass note for both the I and IV chords.

- "Funk" bass lines (octaves) prominently appear in measures 17, 22, and 29. "Pedal tones" and short, walking lines are interwoven throughout.

◆ FUNK #1

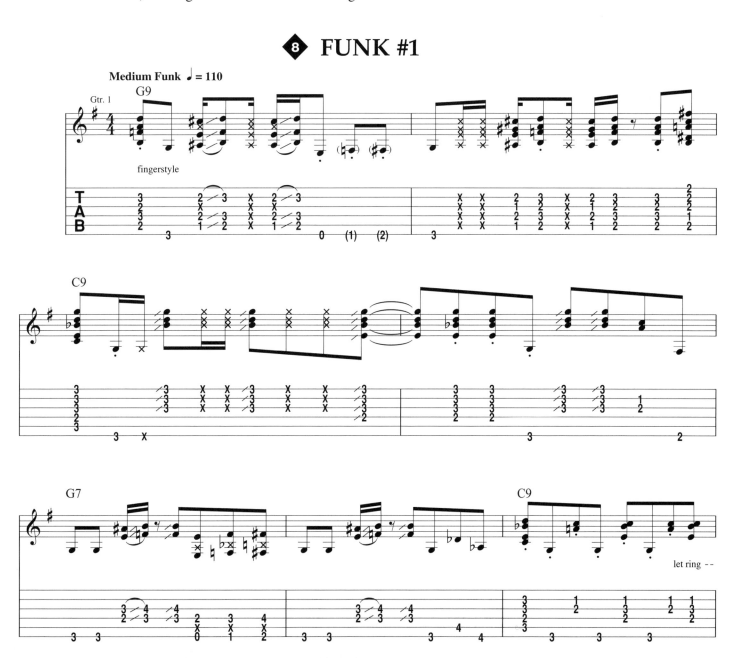

*Fretted with thumb.

Funk #2

Funk #2 is also a I-IV vamp, but this time I have put an improvised solo on top. The rhythm of the drums and bass is very syncopated, while the rhythm guitar pretty much just lays in the groove. I then weave in and out with the lead guitar, always leaving space for the rest of the music to come through.

Musical Analysis

- The I (E7) and IV (A7) chords are played for one measure each throughout.

- The E composite blues scale is used in all five boxes (positions) from the open strings to the octave. Here are the 4th and 5th positions. (See "Blues Scale" chapter for the first three positions.)

4th Position   5th Position

- There are full step bends of the ♭7th to the root, the 4th to the 5th, and the 2nd to the 3rd throughout. In addition, there are numerous quarter step bends from the ♭3rd and ♭7th.

- Measure 32 contains three chromatic unison bends.

- Measures 37-43 contain sliding 6th/9th-interval double stops that follow the I-IV changes.

◆9 FUNK #2

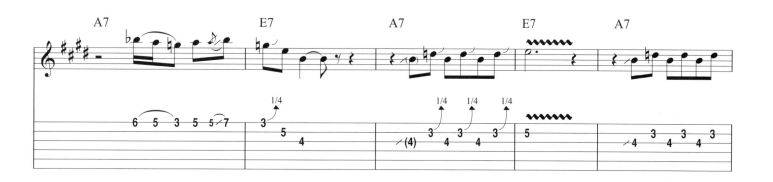

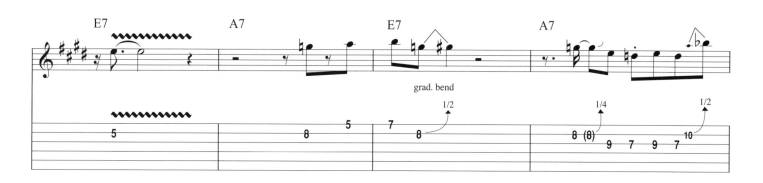

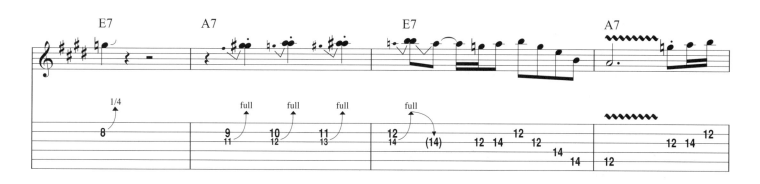

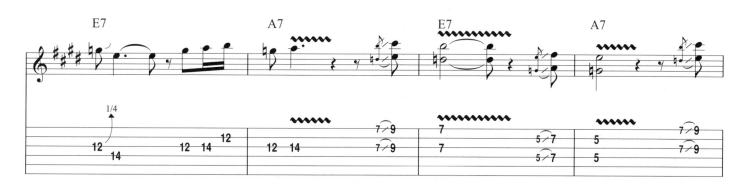

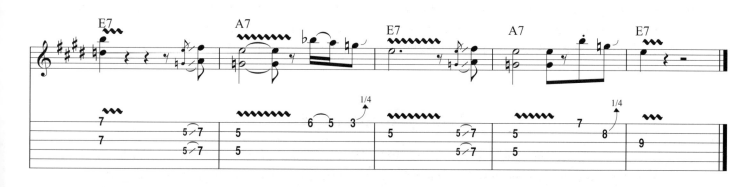

Funk #3

This is basic and classic funk. There is only one chord, an E7, throughout the entire song. The whole point is "phrasing" rather than "filling." When your part in a song calls for playing a groove, you need to know how to maintain it. Keeping it simple is always best, but you must put feeling into it as well. Learn how to accompany well and you will be on everybody's "first call" list.

Musical Analysis

- The one (I) chord played throughout is an E7 form derived from an open C7 voicing, with the 5th (B) on the low E string. On roughly every other beat, an E6 is implied by the lowering of the $\flat$7th (D) to the 6th (C$\sharp$). This can be accomplished by flattening the middle finger to cover the C$\sharp$ note at fret 6 on string 3, as well as the G$\sharp$ note at fret 6 on string 4.

- E6 inversions on the top three strings occur in measures 6, 7, and 24.

- Double stops implying an alternate E7 voicing occur in measures 10 and 14.

- A "reverse turnaround" double-stop pattern appears in measure 20 as an accent. The same pattern is harmonized to 3- and 4-note chord voicings in measure 30, and played in descending order to resolve the song to the I chord.

 **FUNK #3**

58

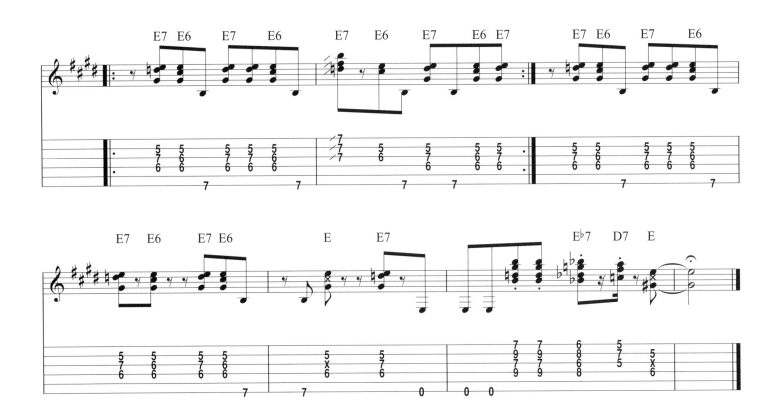

Cornell Remembers...

I have had the great honor to play with many legendary blues, R&B, soul, rock, and pop performers during my long career. Each one had something special to offer and I tried to learn from each experience.

King Curtis

When I came to New York in 1962 to join Curtis I really wasn't that familiar with his music, except for some of the songs he had out at that time like "Soul Twist." We got together, and I sat down with him and "tinked around" on my guitar. He showed me little hooks and "curlicues," and how to listen to the music itself and be a part of it. I look at him as my "degree" in music. After you played with him you could go out and work with anyone. He was influenced a lot by the guitar in the way he played his saxophone. Many of the licks he played came directly from guitarists he had listened to like Billy Butler, and also from country & western and bluegrass music. Curtis played guitar and he and I performed songs like "Frosty" as a duo on the bandstand. He would bring his own guitar and amp to the gig. We also did Sam Cooke's "Bring It On Home" as a vocal duet in harmony. In fact, Curtis really liked to sing, even though he knew he was limited as a vocalist. He loved Ray Charles and would do "What'd I Say," as well as several Marvin Gaye songs. On top of that, he wrote a couple of songs with Shirley Alston of the Shirelles.

Curtis was an original. He developed that "yakety sax" sound that you hear on the Coasters' "Yakety Yak." Another performer named Boots Randolph "borrowed" that sound and put out a record called *Yakety Sax* and ended up getting most of the credit for the sound. Saxophonists whom he admired were Lester Young, Clifford Scott (who played on Bill Doggett's "Honky Tonk" along with Billy Butler), and Stanley Turrentine.

He didn't tell people what to play unless he had something specific in mind. He would just let you play and go along with the music. If it was something that wasn't happening he would mention it, of course. But, if it was sounding good and feeling good, he would let you go and let you create.

One thing he used to say was, "If you can't hear the guy playing next to you, you're playing too loud." He hated loud music and I'm like that today!

Jimi Hendrix

Jimi was already playing loud back then and it was the one thing that kind of irritated Curtis, although he let him go along and do his thing. It was just his style and the loudness went with it. I pretty much played rhythm with Jimi because he wasn't a rhythm guitarist at that time. I had been with Curtis for a few years at this point, so I knew the songs and arrangements better anyway. Jimi would do his picking and little fills here and there. Occasionally, I would play fills when there was room for it; I would not clutter up things. We made it blend and you could hear all the parts making one good sound.

One time the King Curtis band was backing up Chuck Berry at some upstate New York college, and I think Jimi was taking away most of the attention from Chuck. Nothing was said directly to Jimi about it, but I am sure that Chuck did not appreciate it. I remember when we would go out on the road for a couple of days and Jimi would only bring his toothbrush and a shirt, and that would be his wardrobe. *(Laughs)*

Jimi knew the blues and he loved them. Albert King influenced both of us, and I think you can hear that in his playing. He really loved down home blues like Elmore James, although he didn't play too much of that on the bandstand in his sets.

He played the Strat when he was with Curtis, but I never liked that guitar. I played a Guild Starfire at that time and we both had Fender Twin amplifiers. The only effect that he was using was a wah-wah pedal, but the tones he got from his amp were unique. One thing that he did—which I paid attention to—was always use a touch of reverb to make the notes stand out. Before that, I had always had a dry and flat sound.

At the time, I had no idea that he would become as big as he did. He was very timid and shy, and it was hard to see him stepping out and taking charge of things. His personality just didn't project that.

Billy Butler

I was familiar with his playing on "Honky Tonk" because I had learned it note for note, but when I came to New York and heard some of the other recordings that he performed on, I appreciated him even more. I loved his beautiful tone, touch, and "diction." Meeting him and playing along side of him was just incredible. I picked up on a few of his licks from being around him and listening to him. The guitar parts on "Soul Twist" were his creation.

Since I was the "regular" with Curtis when Billy came in, I would assume the rhythm and he would add licks and solos. There was never any real distinction made between who would play what part, unless he had an idea for something specific. We would just play, enjoy, and listen to one another.

He didn't play like the normal R&B guitarist. He wasn't into string bending as much as pretty chords; he enjoyed standards and ballads. Nobody else sounded like Billy Butler. He was unique.

Big Joe Turner

Around 1960, I played a number of dates with Big Joe and Jimmy "T-99" Nelson in the Ft. Worth area with some of my "homeboys." Before every gig he would get a fifth of Scotch, and when he would get to the bandstand someone in the group would play a "C" for him. Then he would sing in the key of C the whole night, except for one song that he would sing in F. He was some singer, with a big strong voice.

Ray Sharpe

Ray was a couple of years older than me. When we were in school, he used to perform at the talent shows and we would call him "hillbilly" because he would yodel. I think he really should have gotten into country & western music—he would have been as big as Charley Pride. Instead, he went into a pop rock style of music. He always had a nice little band around the Ft. Worth/Dallas area and had a hit in 1959 with "Linda Lu."

Ray was a stylist, in a sense. He played blues-rock, as opposed to the down home, "dirty" blues. It always sounded more "pop," with a hint of country & western. Again, I think everyone growing up in those days had to be influenced some by country & western music because that's basically all you heard on the radio.

Bobby Womack

I first met Bobby in Philadelphia on a show that he was playing with his brothers. We were there at a big theater for a week with Sam Cooke. We would sit around and "lollygag" between shows, although we didn't do a lot of playing together. He was left-handed and didn't do a lot of picking. He played chords and fills at the same time, and did these sliding kind of licks that were hard to comprehend *(Laughs)*. Some years after Sam Cooke's death, around 1972, I did a recording in L.A. with Bobby. Cooke's singing heavily influenced him. I haven't seen him in over twenty years. He is still very popular down in Texas where they really liked his recording "Harry Hippie."

Sam Cooke

He was incredible to work with and had a certain ambiance, or a kind of "vibration" about him when he walked onstage. You would get cold chills during some of the songs he would sing. He came from gospel music and he would express that in his songs. I think he was coerced by his management into singing more pop-oriented songs so that he could crossover to the white audience. He was very comfortable with what he had been doing, and I think he lost all that feeling when they tried to get too "pop" with him. I don't think he ever got that far into the white market anyway-he just "touched it" briefly. Sweet, lovely songs like "You Send Me" told cute little stories but did not have that deep feel.

Jerry Wexler

I loved Jerry. I can remember in the beginning, before I even had a phone, he used to send me telegrams to tell me to come to certain sessions. He would call me in as a "trouble-shooter" when things weren't going right. I would always play pretty much what I wanted, whether it was the rhythm or fills or whatever would come to mind. It would usually be done live, although occasionally there would be some overdubs. There was always another guitarist who would be present to play backbeats or something like that. Besides me, he liked Duane Allman and Steve Cropper. From Muscle Shoals, Alabama to Criteria Studios in Miami, as well as sessions here in New York, I was busy. I became very close with Jerry and Arif Mardin at Atlantic.

Jerry was around blues and R&B music for so many years that he knew what he wanted when he heard it. Also, he was able to bring the right people together to produce it. He had a great love for the music.

Steve Cropper

Everything he did, especially with Otis Redding, were the right things for the song. His solos with Booker T just fit the scene at the time and I admired that. It's not that he was such a great player or soloist, but his solos stood out and matched the song.

Ike Turner

I had dinner at Ike and Tina's home in 1965 with Curtis, Chuck Rainey and Norman Douglas. We were in L.A. to play the Hollywood Bowl with the Beatles and were invited to dinner with the Turners. I have never talked with Ike to any extent, but he and Curtis were friends.

He always says that he doesn't consider himself a guitarist but a keyboard player, and I would agree. When he was with Tina he didn't show me anything to make me think he was a guitarist. He was just "there." *(Laughs)*

Eric Gale

Eric was one of the originators of the style of playing rhythm and lead licks at the same time, and he and I played similarly. He was older than me and influenced the way I play rhythms and licks. He turned me on to a lot of sessions that he could not make when I came to New York. Sometimes he would tell me that I would have to read on some sessions, and he would always make sure that I could handle it. If it were simple enough, I could read it down. He never sent me out to do anything that would embarrass him or me.

We worked great together. We never rehearsed or even discussed who would play what part, and it would come out perfect every time. It was always spontaneous, even when we were with Stuff.

James Jamerson

I met James at the Apollo Theater around 1964. He used to come there quite often with Motown acts like Smokey Robinson and the Miracles, the Temptations, the Four Tops, and the Supremes. I played with him once when I was with Aretha at Avery Fisher Hall at Lincoln Center. It was interesting because he did not play what any of the other bass players did. *(Laughs)* It was good, but sometimes it would throw you off when he would play something different from what you were used to hearing another way so many times. He was a fine gentleman and a terrific musician. He was the originator of that particular sound, and his approach to rhythms and technique made Motown what it was. He was kind of busy on the bass most of the time. One of the busiest lines he ever played was on Stevie Wonder's "Signed, Sealed and Delivered." He influenced everybody from Chuck Rainey to, probably, Ron Carter.

I have heard that Motown sometimes used two bass players, with one holding the bottom down while Jamerson did his thing, and it may be true. (Jamerson sometimes overdubbed an upright acoustic bass part.—Ed.) They did use three guitar players, with each one playing a particular part, whether it was the backbeats or the "chicks." ("Chicks" are muted, percussive accents on the guitar strings—Ed.) I once played a session with Carl Lynch and he was the "chick" man. He could play "two" and "four" like no one else could. *(Laughs)*

Lloyd Price

I did some concerts and recordings with Lloyd. In addition, I worked with him at Birdland when he took it over in the late sixties. He used to tell tales about Wilson Pickett when they both lived in Teaneck, New Jersey. There were a couple of occasions when Pickett would come home a little "juiced" and would throw up in Lloyd's yard and drive all over his flowers, messing up his yard. Then he would get out and leave his car where it stopped.

Wilson Pickett

Wilson was a character. He used to drink a "little bit" and would get carried away with his sense of humor and bad temper. He didn't mind speaking out about anything, and he would jump in your face. *(Laughs)* He was fine in the studio, however, and always treated me well. Jerry Wexler or someone else would write out the arrangements, and Wilson would listen to them and "sing down." If something was irritating him he would speak out, but most of the time we would just play, lay the tracks down, and it would go fairly smoothly. Usually, Wilson would get it in one or two takes.

At that time, he was young and strong and his lungs were powerful. He would just scream and do his thing.

Brook Benton

Brook would do more takes than anyone else. He would do a song thirty or forty times, and then we would end up using one of the first ones. Also, he was not into the low down blues per se. He was more of a sweet, story-telling kind of singer like Sam Cooke. Brook liked ballads and Nat "King" Cole-type songs.

We had all heard the original demo of "Rainy Night in Georgia" by Tony Joe White in the studio. We sat around and began playing it, giving it a different feel from the country & western style of the original. I remember that we went over it thirty or forty times. *(Laughs)* We finished up and went home and I forgot what I played on the track. When we came back to the studio the next day, everyone was saying that what I had played was just great. I said, "Well, gee, what did I do?" *(Laughs)* We had done so many takes and I had played it differently each time, so I hadn't recalled what I had played. I didn't know what stuck and what didn't. When they played it back, though, it sounded pretty good.

Part of my inspiration was the playing of Curtis Mayfield and Eric Gale. When I was with King Curtis, we backed up Curtis Mayfield and the Impressions with Jerry Butler at the Apollo Theater around 1963-64. I once did some commercials with Mayfield where he wrote the material but did not play. He had a sound like nobody else.

Duane Allman

Duane and I played together on a couple of albums with Herbie Mann. One in particular was Push Push. We used to sit around in the studio between takes and pick and mess around. He and King Curtis were close friends and we went to some parties together. We used to call him "Sky Man" because he liked to get high. He and Delaney Bramlett also hung out and partied together. He was a nice guy and a good player, especially on slide. I saw him a little over a month before his death at Curtis's funeral. (King Curtis died on August 13, 1971 and Duane Allman died on October 29, 1971-Ed.)

Freddie King

I used to see Freddie perform around Ft. Worth in the late fifties and early sixties, but did not get acquainted with him. Then, in 1969, Curtis produced "My Feeling for the Blues" for Freddie and we backed him up. He used a thumbpick, which I used to do too, until I realized that I could do more with the "plectrum." When I was using the thumbpick, though, I also used my forefinger, pretty much like Freddie did with the fingerpick on that finger.

Freddie was a powerful blues player who could pull the strings. When I was with Curtis, we used to do "Hide Away," "The Stumble," and a few other instrumentals that Freddie played. I liked his style—it was great—but I always leaned more towards Albert King and his feel.

Joe Cocker

That was quite an experience to be with Joe, who is a sweetheart. I love his style of singing-Joe has "soul." *(Laughs)* He has a lot of feeling, and the way he expresses it through his vocals, with his voice being the type that it is, makes it even more soulful to me. He loved Ray Charles and knew a lot about soul and R&B singers.

Joe used to drink "a bit" *(Laughs),* but he never missed a performance. He was a nervous and shy person who would often get sick before a gig, and people used to think it was because of the drinking, but it wasn't.

I recorded with him in 1974, and in 1975 we did a tour of Australia. In 1976, we recorded *Stingray,* which was a great album, in Jamaica, and we also did another tour of the States and Canada. One thing about that album: We went out on the road before it was released, due to his management, and it ended up not being a real big album. It got squashed somehow. The band was Gordon Edwards: bass, Richard Tee: keyboards, Albert Lee: guitar, a percussionist, a drummer, and myself. Albert Lee could play! He did that "English country" thing. This basic group became Stuff a little while later.

When I was in L.A. in 1982-83, I went out to see Joe on the Fonda's farm where he would stay. I haven't seen him since then, but he looks good when I see him on TV, and I understand that he has gotten married and is doing well. I am very happy for him.

Aretha Franklin

She's another one who is a sweetheart, but don't rub her the wrong way! *(Laughs)* I admire her. In the studio, she had a very unorthodox way of playing her chords on the piano. Usually, the only person who could write out what she was playing was Richard Tee. When she would bring in songs, she would first sit down with Richard and show him what she was playing so that he could write out the chords for the rest of us.

Arif Mardin could never figure out what she was playing or how she was voicing the chords. After we had the chords down, we never had a problem in playing the songs.

She was self-taught and unorthodox in her playing, pretty much like me. *(Laughs)* Once I heard her play, though, it might influence me to play something a particular way. She would let me play or do whatever I wanted to, for the most part, and I would just blend in the best I could. Sometimes she would say, "Well, Dupree, instead of doing that right there, why don't you do this at the beginning or at another spot." Maybe I would start playing a lick and she would say, "Yeah, I like that. Do that after I do this here." Her suggestions were always good. I was with her from 1969 to 1975 along with Bernard Purdie: drums, Jerry Jemmott or Chuck Rainey: bass, Truman Thomas: keyboards, Pancho Morales: conga drums, and King Curtis as the bandleader. When we played big halls like the Fillmore, we would hire other horn players. The Fillmore was phenomenal, with Tower of Power opening the show.

Jerry Jemmott and Bernard Purdie

Jerry "Jakey" Jemmott is another unorthodox player who was influenced by horns—trumpets in particular. He gets licks from horn players and again, he is someone with a unique styling. He is unpredictable, *(Laughs)* and someone who can make things happen by doing odd licks here and there. But, they would almost always fit. He is a good guy who is straight-forward, but is also a very dominant player. He takes charge of the rhythm section. I remember on a few occasions he and Bernard Purdie would "clash" about one thing or another. But again, Bernard would clash with anyone, especially when it would come to the rhythms or what not, because he wants to take over and you just can't do that. He wants to be the star of the show and featured on everything. He forgets that he is playing with other people, and you can't do that. Quite often he has bumped heads with different rhythm players, including myself, Chuck Rainey, and everyone who has played with him, because of the attitude he has on the bandstand. But, we get along. I cuss him out and tell him what I want and usually it clears up and we go on to do the session or the concert. He knows it, because I have been telling him for the last twenty years that if he loses a hundred pounds I am going to whup his ass! *(Laughs)* Also, he claims to have played on some Beatles recordings, but it is not true. He just stretches the truth.

When he (Purdie) is on, though, you cannot beat him. He is a great "fat back" drummer, like a machine. You just plug him in and "pow," you've got it. He plays his butt off, which he did at the Fillmore, especially. I admire him for that.

Tom Jones

I love him and he is a hard working man. I did an album with him in the mid-nineties that unfortunately has not been released. We went out to Las Vegas first to catch his show for about three or four days and partied with him and had a good time. It was real nice, and he was most hospitable. On the recording, there was a bunch of old blues songs, and he sang his butt off on every take. While running the songs down while the band was getting together, Tom would get in the booth and sing the song down every time. He can sing, and I admire him for the way he works. He loves the blues and soul, and he would talk about everybody from Lightnin' Hopkins to Brook Benton to Ray Charles to Otis Redding. I loved working with him and he is a fine gentleman.

Harry Belafonte

I played Caesar's Palace Vegas with Harry around 1970. He usually did not have much to say unless a show was not performed exactly as rehearsed. If you did anything differently, it would throw him off and irritate him. He did not want people to "ad lib" too much. It was beautiful being with him, though, and everything was first class all the way.

Lena Horne

I had the pleasure of recording with her and Gato Barbieri, Eric Gale, Richard Tee, Grady Tate, and a big band. I admire her singing and her character very much.

Sarah Vaughan

I did a commercial one time with Sarah. When Stuff used to play at Mikell's in New York, she would come by and sit in. She is a fine, funny lady who cracks jokes and cusses like a sailor! *(Laughs)*

Barbra Streisand

Along with Gordon Edwards and Eric Gale, I recorded an album called *Guilty* with Barbra around 1980. We went to Criteria Studios in Miami to provide that "Stuff sound" for her. After we ran down a few songs, however, they changed their mind as to using the whole group. I think it was a little too funky. It ended up that just Richard Tee and I, along with some local musicians, did the album. Barry Gibb wrote most of the songs, as well as producing and arranging the project. I always liked for the artist to sing the songs before we recorded, and Barbra did sing them down for us. I never had a specific thing in mind to play until I heard the melody and the way a singer would do a song. The session went very smoothly.

The songs were kind of pop rock with a slightly funky flavor. It was a good album, although not one of her biggest sellers. It was nice working with her, and a very pleasant occasion.

Mariah Carey

Around 1990, I did some overdubs and fills on three songs on a recording project. I remember asking Mariah what she wanted me to play on her songs and she said, "Do some of that stuff that you did on Aretha's records." I said, "No problem." Again, I requested that she would sing along so that I would know what the song was about. It was a very pleasant couple of hours. She has a big voice for a little lady.

Cornell's Equipment Set-up

Guitars

Most of the guitars that I first played did not record clearly. I don't know if it was the way I was playing them or the guitars themselves. As I changed guitars, though, my sound started getting a little more distinct, especially the chords. Half of it may have been the way I was fingering the chords, so that some of the notes did not ring out. This was true from the Gibson Les Paul to the Guild Starfire to the Standel. King Curtis used to tell me, "Change guitars. Try this one, try that one." Around 1969-70, I changed to Fender and the notes and chords were clearer. The first Fender that I owned was a Tele. I stuck with it up until the time I got with Yamaha. The Yamahas that I endorse and play are like a Japanese Telecaster. On my particular Telecaster, I had added a DeArmond pickup in the center position that I had removed from my Guild Starfire. Up until that time, I had always felt that my sound was thin. What I liked about the DeArmond was that it had "balls" and "bite," and I was pretty much satisfied with the results. On my second or third trip to Japan, Yamaha noticed my guitar and made one for me in the likeness of my Tele. Around 1977, they made up a few of them for me, called the Dupree Super Jam, and I have been playing Yamahas ever since. Just recently, I endorsed the new Cornell Dupree Signature guitar and I am really in love with it.

Strings

I use the following Yamaha string gauges: .010, .013, .016, .026, .032, .037. My bottom E string is light, but heavy enough to play a chord. With too light of a string you can tune your guitar to an open chord, but as soon as you go up the neck for a chord, you will pull on the string and it will go out of tune. I play hard and really grab the strings so that my notes are "enunciated." I like to dig in, especially for those quarter-step bends.

Amps

I started off playing Fender Twin Reverbs and now I play Yamaha Twins. They are tube amps and they come across for me. They "predict" what I put in, tone-wise, and are fitting for what I play. I don't play loud so I don't have to worry about power. Also, I do not use effects. All I want is a nice, clean, full tone. When I want a raunchy sound, the guitar projects pretty much what I want and does what I tell it to do.

Cornell at the Zanzibar in New York City, February, 1994

Selected Discography

Cornell Dupree has appeared on over 2,500 record dates. Listed below are a fraction of these sessions that are currently available.

Solo:

Teasin' Atlantic
Shadow Dancing MSG
Guitar Groove Topline
Coast to Coast Antilles
Can't Get Through Amazing
Child's Play Amazing
Bop 'n' Blues Kokopelli
Uncle Funky (live) Kokopelli
Unstuffed Import
Double Clutch Meteor

With King Curtis:

Blow Man Blow
Best of King Curtis
Live at Small's Paradise
Instant Groove
Live at Fillmore West
Blues at Montreux
Instant Soul
King Curtis & the Kingpins

With Aretha Franklin:

Spirit in the Dark
Aretha Live at Fillmore West
Young, Gifted and Black
Amazing Grace
With Everything I Feel
Let Me in Your Life
La Diva
30 Greatest Hits
Aretha
Queen of Soul: The Atlantic Recordings
Greatest Hits (1980-1994)
Amazing Grace; The Complete Recordings

With Stuff:

Stuff
More Stuff
Stuff It
Live in New York
Right Stuff

With Others:

Atlantic Jazz
Great Jazz Vocalists Sing Strayhorn
Every Village Has a Song (Yusef Lateef)
Anthology (Yusef Lateef)
Genius & Soul: The 50th Anniversary (Ray Charles)
House of David: The David "Fathead" Newman Band (David "Fathead" Newman)
Lonely Avenue (David "Fathead" Newman)
Scratch My Back (David "Fathead" Newman)
Return to the Wide Open Spaces (David "Fathead" Newman)
Heart and Soul (Hank Crawford)
It's A Funky Thing to Do (Hank Crawford)
Help Me Make It Through the Night (Hank Crawford)
We Got a Good Thing Going (Hank Crawford)
Mr. Chips (Hank Crawford)
Evolution of Mann (Herbie Mann)
Push Push (Herbie Mann)
Opalescence (Herbie Mann)
Apollo Saturday Night
In the Midnight Hour (Wilson Pickett)
Prime Element (Elvin Jones)
At This Point in Time (Elvin Jones)
Atlantic Jazz:Fusion
Watch What Happens (Lena Horne)
With Love from Lena (Lena Horne)
New Routes (Lulu)
Live at Freddie Jett's Pied Piper (Esther Phillips)
Best of Stanley Turrentine (Stanley Turrentine)
Cherry (Stanley Turrentine)
Best of Mr. T (Stanley Turrentine)
Man with the Sad Face (Stanley Turrentine)
Christmas and the Beads of Sweat (Laura Nyro)
My Feeling for the Blues (Freddie King)
Donny Hathaway (Donny Hathaway)
Live (Donny Hathaway)
Extension of a Man (Donny Hathaway)
Best of Donny Hathaway (Donny Hathaway)
Upfront (David Sanborn)
Portrait of the Blues (Lou Rawls)
At Last (Lou Rawls)
Ballads (Lou Rawls)
It's Supposed to be Fun (Lou Rawls)
Legendary Lou Rawls (Lou Rawls)
Blue Boat (Vig Steen)

1964-1993 (Paul Simon)
There Goes Rhymin' Simon (Paul Simon)
Otis! The Definitive Otis Redding (Otis Redding)
Atlantic Jazz: Saxophone (Atlantic Jazz: Saxophone)
Atlantic Jazz: Saxophones, Vol. 2
    (Atlantic Jazz: Saxophone)
Golden Soul Classics (Joneses)
Keepin' Up with the Joneses (Joneses)
Best of Candi Staton (Candi Staton)
Young Hearts Run Free (Candi Staton)
Chance (Candi Staton)
Get It While You Can (Howard Tate)
Blues Masters, Vols. 1-5 (Blues Masters)
Way I Feel (Nikki Giovanni)
Did You Hear Me(Rufus Thomas)
Crown Prince of Dance (Rufus Thomas)
Sax for Lovers (Sax for Lovers)
New Groove: The Blue Note Remix
    (New Groove: The Blue Note Remix)
Best of Grover Washington, Jr. (Grover Washington, Jr.)
All the King's Horses (Grover Washington, Jr.)
Fritz the Cat/Heavy Traffic (Fritz the Cat/Heavy Traffic)
Greatest Hits (Loleatta Holloway)
Big Band Masters (Big Band Masters)
Plays Selections from West Side Story (Buddy Rich)
Ease on Down the Road (Buddy Rich)
Big Band Machine (Buddy Rich)
Groovy: A Collection of Rare Club Tracks
    (Groovy: A Collection of Rare Club Tracks)
Stoned Soul Picnic: The Best of Laura Nyro (Laura Nyro)
Best of Esther Phillips (1962-1970) (Esther Phillips)
From a Whisper to a Scream (Esther Phillips)
Alone Again (Naturally) (Esther Phillips)
Burnin'/Confessin' the Blues (Esther Phillips)
Set Me Free (Esther Phillips)
Jackie Robinson Tribute: Stealing Home
    (Jackie Robinson Tribute)
Last Man Standing (MC Eiht)
Kiss My Blues (Tony Z.)
James Brown's Original Funky Divas
    (James Brown's Original Funky Divas)
Reality (James Brown)
Blue Break Beats (Grant Green)
Best of Grant Green, Vol. 2 (Grant Green)
Fool's Parade (Peter Wolf)
Blacknuss (Rahsaan Roland Kirk)
Standing Eight (Rahsaan Roland Kirk)
Case of the 3 Sided Dream in Audio
    (Rahsaan Roland Kirk)
Left Hook, Right Cross (Rahsaan Roland Kirk)
Vibrations Continue (Rahsaan Roland Kirk)
Groovy: Collection of Rare Club Tracks
    (Groovy; Collection of Rare Club Tracks)
Mrs. Magic (Carmen McRae)
Gold Sunrise on Magic Mountain (Leon Thomas)

Blues and the Soulful Truth (Leon Thomas)
You Can't Make Love Alone (Eddie "Cleanhead" Vinson)
Trees and Grass and Things (Charles Williams)
Invitation to Openness (Les McCann)
Soul is... Pretty Purdie (Bernard "Pretty" Purdie)
Guess Who (B.B. King)
King of the Blues (B.B. King)
Get Up with It (Miles Davis)
Attica Blues (Archie Shepp)
Madame Foo Foo (Dakota Staton)
Moonglow (Dakota Staton)
Dakota Staton: Sonny Lester Collection (Dakota Staton)
Of the Three Sounds (Gene Harris)
Marlena (Marlena Shaw)
From the Depths of My Soul(Marlena Shaw)
Best of Marlena Shaw: Blue Note Years (Marlena Shaw)
Live at Sing Sing, Vol. 1 (Eddie Palmieri)
Chuck Rainey Coalition (Chuck Rainey)
Movin' On (Oscar Brown, Jr.)
Super Freak (Pucho & His Latin Soul)
Starring Charlie Allen (Pacific Gas & Electric)
Dynamite Brothers (Charles Earland)
Hustler's Convention (Lightnin' Rod)
Mr. Bojangles (Sonny Stitt)
Bette Midler (Bette Midler)
I Wanna Be Selfish (Ashford & Simpson)
Queen of the Night (Maggie Bell)
Cosmic Vortex (Weldon Irvine)
Creatures of the Street (Jobriath)
Total Eclipse (Billy Cobham)
Sweet Lou (Lou Donaldson)
Anthology, Vol. 2 (Duane Allman)
I Can Stand a Little Rain (Joe Cocker)
Jamaica Say You Will (Joe Cocker)
Joe Cocker's Greatest Hits (Joe Cocker)
Luxury You Can Afford (Joe Cocker)
Journey (Arif Mardin)
Is Having a Wonderful Time (Geoff Muldaur)
RSVP (Zulema)
Margie (Margie Joseph)
Sassy Mama (Big Mama Thorton)
Mama's Pride (Big Mama Thorton)
Spoonful (Jimmy Witherspoon)
Sum of the Parts (Larry Ridley)
All American Alien Boy (Ian Hunter)
Dinner Music (Carla Bley)
Home in the Country (Pee Wee Ellis)
Tymes Up (Tymes)
Stingray (Joe Cocker)
In My Stride (David Ruffin)
Master Grady Tate (Grady Tate)
Ringo the 4th (Ringo Starr)
16 Most Requested Songs (Teresa Brewer)
Warmer Communications... and More
    (Average White Band)

Faith, Hope & Charity (Faith, Hope & Charity)
Kate Taylor (Kate Taylor)
Boys in the Trees (Carly Simon)
One and Only (Gladys Knight)
Deep in the Night (Etta James)
Bottom Line (John Mayall)
Midnight Rendezvous (Tasha Thomas)
Chaka (Chaka Khan)
Ghetto Blaster (Crusaders)
Guilty (Barbra Streisand)
Denon Jazz Sampler, Vol. 1 (Denon Jazz Sampler)
Atlantic Blues: Chicago (Atlantic Blues)
Atlantic Blues: Guitar (Atlantic Blues: Guitar)
Atlantic Blues Box (Atlantic Blues Box)
Camera Never Lies (Michael Franks)
At Home (Janis Siegel)
Watt Works Family Album (Watt Works Family Album)
Best of the Big Bands Vol. 1 (Best of the Big Bands)

Texas Blues (Lightnin' Hopkins)
Emotions (Mariah Carey)
Greatest Hits Collection (Andy Gibb)
Atlantic Rhythm & Blues 1947-1974
   (Atlantic Rhythm & Blues)
Gadd Gang (Gadd Gang)
Mr. Excitement (Jackie Wilson)
Soul of R&B Revue (Soul of R&B Revue)
Never Been Rocked Enough (Delbert McClinton)
Woke Up This Mornin' (LaVern Baker)
Blues Masters, Vol. 3: Texas Blues (Blues Masters)
Change Is Gonna Come (Jack McDuff)
Ellerine (Ellerine Harding)
On the Town (Webster Lewis)
Last Dance (Rosie)
Warren Schatz (Warren Schatz)
Outrageous (Johnnie Pate)

Guitar Notation Legend

Guitar Music can be notated three different ways: on a *musical staff*, in *tablature*, and in *rhythm slashes*.

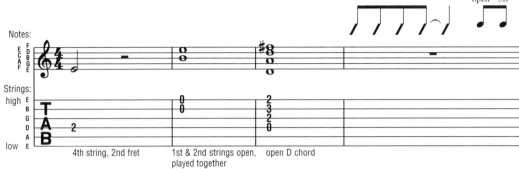

RHYTHM SLASHES are written above the staff. Strum chords in the rhythm indicated. Use the chord diagrams found at the top of the first page of the transcription for the appropriate chord voicings. Round noteheads indicate single notes.

THE MUSICAL STAFF shows pitches and rhythms and is divided by bar lines into measures. Pitches are named after the first seven letters of the alphabet.

TABLATURE graphically represents the guitar fingerboard. Each horizontal line represents a string, and each number represents a fret.

HALF-STEP BEND: Strike the note and bend up 1/2 step.

BEND AND RELEASE: Strike the note and bend up as indicated, then release back to the original note. Only the first note is struck.

HAMMER-ON: Strike the first (lower) note with one finger, then sound the higher note (on the same string) with another finger by fretting it without picking.

TRILL: Very rapidly alternate between the notes indicated by continuously hammering on and pulling off.

PICK SCRAPE: The edge of the pick is rubbed down (or up) the string, producing a scratchy sound.

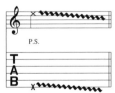

TREMOLO PICKING: The note is picked as rapidly and continuously as possible.

WHOLE-STEP BEND: Strike the note and bend up one step.

PRE-BEND: Bend the note as indicated, then strike it.

PULL-OFF: Place both fingers on the notes to be sounded. Strike the first note and without picking, pull the finger off to sound the second (lower) note.

TAPPING: Hammer ("tap") the fret indicated with the pick-hand index or middle finger and pull off to the note fretted by the fret hand.

MUFFLED STRINGS: A percussive sound is produced by laying the fret hand across the string(s) without depressing, and striking them with the pick hand.

VIBRATO BAR DIVE AND RETURN: The pitch of the note or chord is dropped a specified number of steps (in rhythm) then returned to the original pitch.

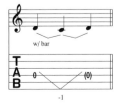

GRACE NOTE BEND: Strike the note and immediately bend up as indicated.

VIBRATO: The string is vibrated by rapidly bending and releasing the note with the fretting hand.

LEGATO SLIDE: Strike the first note and then slide the same fret-hand finger up or down to the second note. The second note is not struck.

NATURAL HARMONIC: Strike the note while the fret-hand lightly touches the string directly over the fret indicated.

PALM MUTING: The note is partially muted by the pick hand lightly touching the string(s) just before the bridge.

VIBRATO BAR SCOOP: Depress the bar just before striking the note, then quickly release the bar.

SLIGHT (MICROTONE) BEND: Strike the note and bend up 1/4 step.

WIDE VIBRATO: The pitch is varied to a greater degree by vibrating with the fretting hand.

SHIFT SLIDE: Same as legato slide, except the second note is struck.

PINCH HARMONIC: The note is fretted normally and a harmonic is produced by adding the edge of the thumb or the tip of the index finger of the pick hand to the normal pick attack.

RAKE: Drag the pick across the strings indicated with a single motion.

VIBRATO BAR DIP: Strike the note and then immediately drop a specified number of steps, then release back to the original pitch.